CONTENTS

Mythology, which is made up of the combination of 'mythos' meaning 'narrated or heard word' and 'logos' meaning 'speech', in Greek, can be defined as the study of legends dealing with the stories of the heroes, deities or supernatural creatures in the culture of a religion or a people, stretching over thousands of years.

At times, humankind interpreted the universe, earth and natural events by attributing them to people, creating various myths to express life and natural events that puzzled them. These stories and legends were enriched by adopting from each other over centuries and thus the legends exist to this day. These legends, which are centered mainly around gods, goddesses and superhuman heroes, became a source of inspiration for many branches of art too.

The fact that every nation and country had its own distinct culture allowed mythology to be nourished by these cultures and caused variations according to the location. The mythologies of Egypt, Phoenicia and Mesopotamia passed down to Anatolia over time, merged here with the Hittite culture and reached as far as Greece through the islands. Greek mythology today owes its prominence to the major role played by the Greek and Roman authors who recorded these myths in writing. Most of these myths, with many Anatolian characters, began to develop in Anatolia.

Homer and Hesiod are the major sources giving account of these legends, and mythology began to be written with these authors. Homer of Ioania was born around 850 BC, somewhere around the banks of the River Meles in Smyrna. He was originally named Melesigenes, which alluded to his place of birth, but was later named *Homer* when he was taken hostage by the Chiosians.

Homer is known to have collected the stories of the Trojan War from the 9th through 8th century BC. In his epic Iliad, Homer tells

Homer, a poet of İzmir, who wrote the Iliad around 750 BC.

ΣΚΗΝΗ   ΕΥΡΕ

*Embossment carved
in the honor of Euripides.
Late Hellenistic, early Roman Period.
(1st century BC-1st century AD Smyrna)*

of the last 51 days of the Trojan War which lasted for ten years.
This epic poem is made up of 16,000 verses and 24 chapters. As
much as he was a great minstrel, Homer was a good observer too.
His geographical depictions of where the war took place are
remarkably close to reality even today. This epic, which precedes

Homer's Odyssey, begins with the conflict between Agamemnon and Achilles and ends with the death of Hector. Homer's Odyssey tells of the sea adventures of King Odysseus of Ithaca. Homer's epic stories are set in Greek cities and even though Homer's heart was inclined towards the Trojans, his expressionism intrinsically emphasizes the Achaean characters. An order given towards 550 BC, by Peisistratus, the tyrant of Athens, that Homer's stories be recorded in writing ensured the place of these oral narratives in history.

Hesiod, who lived around 700 BC, stands out as the most important minstrel of antiquity after Homer. Hesiod is the author of "Works and Days" and "Theogony".

Hesiod lived about two centuries after Homer, in the Aeolian city of Cyme. His father was a sailor and carried freight with his ships. Due to poverty, he left his hometown and migrated to the city of Astra in the Boeotia region of Greece. Hesiod grew up but he left his heart in the Aegean. Because he longed for the Aegean, his language and all the elements in his works come from Aeolia and Ionia. Hesiod's "Works and Days" deals with the onerous living conditions of the poor peasants of the period, while "Theogony" features the formation of the universe, creation of humankind, Prometheus, who gave the gift of fire to humankind; giants and Zeus's marriages.

The third most important great epic in our book is Virgil's epic of Aeneid. Publius Vergilius Maro (Virgil) was born in 70 BC, in Andes of Montua, Italy. He began to write the Aeneid in 29 BC. It tells of the voyage of Prince Aeneas, who was a cousin of Hector of Troy, to Italian coasts together with a group of Trojans who were able to escape the devastation of Troy.

Virgil was not able to complete this epic poem made up of 12 chapters even ten years after he began to write it. The poet, who died in 19 BC, without being able to complete his epic, requested before his death that the poem be burnt; however, Emperor Augustus ordered that the work be printed. Author Titus Livius (59 BC-AD 17) continued the epic which Virgil left unfinished and completed it in his work known as the Roman History.

Whereas these epics revolve around the Trojan War, many

independent stories that took place before and after this war were also told by many antiquity authors. Paris's birth, Paris's judgement, and Helen's abduction to Troy are also to be encountered in the works of Euripides and Apollodorus. The events which took place during the Trojan expedition set by the Achaeans are told in the "Iphigenia in Aulis" of Euripides. This work of Euripides deals with the sacrifice of Iphigenia, the daughter of Agamemnon and Clytemnestra in Greek mythology, to Artemis by her father in return for the wind, which was needed by the Achaean ships setting out for the Trojan War. As stated previously, we learn about the events that took place during the war from the Iliad of Homer.

Sophocles, who lived from 497-407 BC, treats the events that took place during the ten-year resistance of Troy in his work "Aias". This prolific subject was told in some important works such as Aias and Philoctetes by Sophocles, Andromache by Racine, and Bibliotheca by Apollodorus. We learn about the events that took place after Troy from the "Trojan Women" and "Hecuba" by Euripides and from "Agamemnon" by Aeschylus, who lived from 525-455 BC, and is considered to be the father of tragedy.

Oedipus's tragic story, which is one of the subjects highlighted the most in mythology, was written by Sophocles. Apollonius of Rhodes, who headed the Library of Alexandria in the 3rd century BC, wrote "The Argonauts", which is almost on the same level as the works of Homer.

Ovid, who lived from 43 BC-17, tells of the myth of Eros (Amor) and Psyche in his work "Metamorphoses". Apollodorus of Athens, who lived around 150 BC, wrote some commentaries on the Iliad.

These mythological subjects, which were taken up by many authors and thinkers in the past, consist of episodic and vivid accounts which complement each other. Bringing together the enchanting myths of antiquity within a sequence and unity embodies the thousands-of-years-old story of the geography we inhabit.

THE CREATION OF THE UNIVERSE AND THE ORIGIN OF DEITIES

According to Hesiod's Theogony, the first formation, namely the beginning of the universe, was chaos which meant uncertainty, infinite emptiness or disorder.

From chaos, Gaia (the Mother Earth) emerged. The Earth, which formed the foundation, was a universal mother giving birth to everything. After this, Eros, the basis of love and symbol of reproduction, and Tartarus, the deepest place of the land of the dead, were born. Subsequently, Erebus, the darkness of the underworld and Nyx, the darkness of the night originated. The two of them merged and formed Aether, the light of heavens and Hemera, the light of terrestrial regions.

Gaia is the main principle found at the source of all elements. She created the Heaven (Uranus), the sea (Pontus) and the mountains. From the union of Mother Earth with Uranus, 6 male and 6 female, a total of 12 Titans were born, along with three Cyclopes named Brontes, Steropes and Arges, who were supernatural beings with a single round eye on their foreheads and could govern lightning, thunder and sky. Again from her union with Uranus, the Hecatonchires named Cottos, Briareus and Gyes were born, who were violent giants with a hundred arms.

As the Titans were born, Uranus feared that he would be deprived of his power and thus dumped them in the depths of the ground. Deeply grieved by this, Gaia plotted a cunning scheme together with her sons and had the last remaining Titan Cronus cut his father's genitals. The blood spurting from him diffused on the Earth and impregnated it. Time went by and the Earth bore the Erinyes the goddesses of retribution, the Gigantes (giants), and the Nymphs who were woodland fairies.

The genitals, which were thrown into the sea, created sea foam, resulting in the creation of Aphrodite. Therefore, Cronus's rule began and the development of the universe continued. Nyx continued to reproduce by herself. Her creations were dark powers symbolizing evil,

Tethys, the wife of Oceanus. The mosaic, which was found in Antakya, is exhibited at the Baltimore Museum of Art in the USA today.

Overleaf: The floor mosaic showing Oceanus and his wife Tethys. It was found in Zeugma and is exhibited at Gaziantep Museum today.

hunger, devastation and death. These were Thanatos (death), Hypnos (sleep), the Hesperides, and the three Moirae named Clotho, Lachesis, Atropos, and Nemesis who caused excessive self confidence, and Eris the goddess of strife.

From the union of Mother Earth with the sea (Pontus) came forth the sea gods Thaumas, Phorcys and Nereus and the goddesses Ceto and Eurybia.

The 50 daughters of Nereus were born from the union of Nereus and Doris, daughter of Oceanus (the father of rivers). From the union of Electra, another daughter of Oceanus, and Thaumas, who was one of the sons of Gaia, came forth Iris who symbolized the rainbow and was associated with communication, and the Harpies which had women's faces, wings and sharp claws.

From the union of Phorcys and his sister Ceto came forth the Graeae and Gorgons who were old women from their birth. Of these Gorgons named Stheno, Euryale and Medusa, only Medusa was mortal. Perseus beheaded Medusa and from her blood shed on the ground emerged Pegasus, the winged horse, and Chrysaor. Chrysaor and Oceanus's daughter Callirrhoe married and begat Geryones, who was a giant with three heads, and Echidna, who was an enormous half-woman, half-snake monster. Echidna's union with giant Typhoon brought forth Cerberus the dog of Hades, Hydra the swamp monster, and fire-breathing monsters such as Chimera.

Titans

The first thing Cronus did was to save his siblings who were placed underground by his father. Cronus's brother Oceanus and Tethys united and from this union came forth three thousand river gods, and three thousand female beings which were to be named the daughters of Oceanus. Titan Hyperion married his sister Thea. From this marriage Helios (the Sun), Selene (the Moon) and Eos (dawn) were born. Crios united with Eurybia, the daughter of the earth and sea, and from this union came forth Astraeus, Pallas and Perses. The union of Astraeus and Eos, the goddess of dawn, produced the winds.

Titan Coeus married his sister Phoebe and from this marriage Leto and Asteria, the star goddess, were born. Another Titan Iapetus married Oceanus's daughter Clymene and their offsprings were Atlas, Menoetius, Epimetheus and Prometheus who each became a subject of legends.

Cronus married his sister Rhea and from this marriage came forth the third-generation Olympian gods. These were Hestia, Demeter, Hera, Poseidon, Hades and Zeus.

Cronus, who attained power by killing his father, feared that his children would do the same thing and thus began to swallow his newborn children. Hestia, Demeter, Hera, Hades and Poseidon were in their father's stomach. This made Rhea very sad but she did not know how to help, until she thought of a cunning trick when her last child Zeus was born.

When the baby came into the world, she took him to Crete in the darkness of the night and hid him in a cave in the depths of a forest. She deceived her husband Cronus by wrapping a stone and presenting it as the newborn. The Curetes slammed their shields together and danced so that the sound of the crying baby in the cave would not be heard by his father. The baby was fed by the Nymph Amalthea with goat's milk and grew up in the fresh forest air. Thus he thrived day by day and became a young man. Finally, he took action against his father Cronus and saved his siblings by making him throw up all of the children that he had swallowed, one by one. He imprisoned his father in the depths of the ground. Zeus was forming the third-generation of gods in Olympus, while Cronus's Titan siblings were waging war against Zeus.

The Titans were divided into two. Oceanus, Hyperion, Themis and Mnemosyne sided with Zeus. The second-generation Titans such as Prometheus and his brother Epimetheus remained unbiased. Zeus went underground and released the Hecatonchires with hundred arms and the Cyclopes the single eyed giants, who were all chained underground. The Titans were fighting from Mount Othrys and Zeus was fighting from Mount Olympus. They threw large stones at each other. The giants with hundred arms, who were on the side of Zeus, were throwing 300 stones at them at one time. When the war continued at full speed, the single-eyed Cyclopes helped Zeus by gifting him with thunder and lightning.

This war named Titanomachia, which was waged in the two high hills of Thessaly, lasted ten years and resulted in Zeus defeating the Titans who were not able to withstand the his thunderbolts. Zeus imprisoned the Titans underground, shackled them and left the hundred-armed giants as guards over them.

Zeus was able to beat the Titans; however, Mother Earth, who could not

stand the defeat of her offsprings, gave birth to a giant monster named Typhoon and made him attack Zeus. Zeus knocked him down with his thunderbolts and declared his dominion in Olympus. Zeus shared the universe with his siblings and formed the Olympian group of gods. He took charge of the sky. He gave Poseidon the sea, Hades the underworld. The Earth and Olympus were accepted as common property. He equipped his other siblings Demeter, Hestia and Hera with multiple powers and took them on as partners to his rule. He had children born from the goddesses he married to and he brought them to Olympus as well and gave them powers.

Gigantes

Hesiod mentions the Gigantes in his Theogony and provides information about them. These were the 24 giants who emerged from the blood shed on the Earth from the genitals of Uranus. Uranus was killed by Cronus in Phleora within the borders of Thrace. Hesiod describes them as

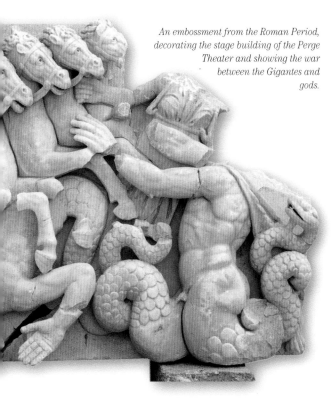

having gleaming armor and long spears. Other authors postdating him also described them as very tall and strong. They were enormous monsters with bodies shaped as a snake and heads shaped as a bull and lion. The Gigantes, the most famous of whom were Alcyoneus, Ephialtes, Eurytos, Thyrso and Enceladus, attacked Olympus by piling mountains one on top of another, to end the rule of the Olympians.

Also engaged in this war were Apollo, Ares, Artemis, Athena, Hephaestus, Hermes, Hecate and even the Moirae. After a prophesy stating that they could only be beaten by a mortal, Zeus called his son Heracles for help, found the magic grass on the Earth and prevented the giants from using it. The giants and the Olympian gods fell upon each other. Apollo the god killed Ephialtes with his famous arrow, and Artemis killed Eurytos. Heracles was chasing Alcyoneus. Each time he slammed the giant on the ground, he gained strength from the earth and stood up again. He was not to be killed on the lands where he was born.

An embossment found in Aphrodisias, showing the war between
the gods and giants and depicting Athena while fighting the giants.
Roman Period. Istanbul Archaeology Museums.

Therefore, Athena advised Heracles that he take him to other lands. So Heracles slung him over his back, took him somewhere else and killed him there with an arrow. Witnessing the defeat, Enceladus had hardly begun to flee when Athena threw the island of Sicily at him. Thus Olympian gods continued their dominion after defeating the Titans, and subsequently the Gigantes, who were another type of giant creatures. The war, which was known as Gigantomachia, waged between the Gigantes and the Olympians for ten years. (Apollodorus, Bibliotheca 1.) Beginning from the 6th century BC, this strife retained its popularity including during the Roman period. This could be seen in a black Athenian vase dating to 550 BC. Additionally, this war has been illustrated in the friezes and embossments of many temples. For instance in Greece, in the Temple of Athena in Corfu, in the Delphi Treasury Building, and the eastern metopes of the Parthenon, this theme is seen. It is also depicted in the metopes of the two temples in Selinus Sicily, which date to the 6-5th centuries BC, on a frieze of the Temple of

Poseidon in Sounion from 5 BC, and on the embossed metopes of Heraion of Argos. In Anatolia, the same theme is featured on the eastern frieze of the Temple of Hecate at Lagina, at the Temple of Athena at Priene, on the embossed gate of the Agora of Aphrodisias. This was also a preferred theme for ceiling frescoes during the Renaissance and Baroque periods. However, the most outstanding illustration of this is seen at the Altar of Zeus in Pergamum (Pergamon). This altar, which was erected in memory of the victory won by King Eumenes II of Pergamum (197-159 BC) against the Galatians, has four stories. It is shaped as a horse shoe, measures 35,64 x 33.40 m. and has a podium with five steps. Above this is a frieze and on the upper-most section is a stoa surrounded by columns. The majestic external staircase to the west is 20 m. wide. The whole building was 10 m. high. Surrounding the building were friezes measuring 120 m. long and are made up of 118 embossments depicting the war between the gods and the Gigantes. The friezes are in the form of high relief and they include all of the gods. All four sides of the altar illustrate the war between the gods and giants as told in Hesiod's Theogony, in the form of high relief and in a manner reflecting the Pergamum sculpture. On the eastern side

An embossment on the eastern frieze of the Altar of Zeus in Pergamum, showing the war between the gods and giants and illustrating Athena fighting the giant Alcyoneus.

are Zeus, Athena, Nike, Ares and after them, Leto, Artemis, Apollo and Hecate. Heracles is situated near Zeus.

On the southern side, Helios the god of Sun is in combat, while his sister Eos, the goddess of dawn, is riding a horse before him. Selene, the Moon Goddess, is following Helios. On the northern side, Nyx, the Goddess of the Night, is fighting. Surrounding her are her relatives Eris the Goddess of Strife, and the Moirae who spread destiny.

On the western side, gods and goddesses relating to the sea such as Poseidon, Amphitrite, Nereus, Doris, Oceanus and Tethys are fighting. On the internal section of the altar, there are friezes of Telephus, the legendary founder of Pergamum. On these friezes, which are made

up of thirty images, the life of Telephus, the son of Heracles and Auge, is described (This will be elaborated on in the section Trojan Expedition I).

Carl Humann, who was in Western Anatolia for the construction of the highway between Ayvalık and Pergamum, recorded that, in 1869, he was in Bergama (Pergamum), where he obtained some pieces on the Pergamum Hill and sent them to Berlin. Later, Professor Alexander Canze, who became the administrator of the Berlin Museum, became the first person to appreciate the value of these pieces. In 1878, the first excavations started in Pergamum. The friezes found here belonging to the Altar of Zeus were shipped to Germany in containers on a ship docked in Dikili. Even though the artifacts were taken to Russia during the Second World War, they were restored at the end of the war. These artifacts were erected again after the building of a museum named Pergamum Museum.

THE CREATION OF HUMANKIND, PROMETHEUS AND PANDORA

Mountains, plains and seas were created, and the universe was filled with deities. But there was no humankind on the earth yet. Hesiod says that the first human generation, the Golden Generation, was seen on earth during the time of Cronus. Following this race, which suddenly disappeared, a second generation was seen after Zeus gained dominance in Olympus. Human beings belonging to this generation, who were known as the Silver Generation and whose childhood lasted for a hundred years, did not respect the gods or visit the temples. Zeus became angry with these people and caused the world to have four different seasons as opposed to one single season, which used to exist until that day. Therefore people had to take shelter in caves in the cold of winter. Yet the tactlessness of these people would not end so Zeus cast them into the underworld and turned them into underground spirits.

Zeus then created a third generation. This generation was the Bronze Generation. Having also destroyed this generation, Zeus later created the Generation of Heroes, and afterwards the Iron Generation. He made them experience fear, sadness and happiness. Titan Iapetus had offsprings with Oceanus's daughter Clymene, which were named Atlas, Menoetios, Epimetheus and Prometheus. Prometheus was seen as helpful and stood beside Zeus.

The other two siblings of Prometheus and their father sided with the Titans. Thus Zeus had slain Menoetios with his thunderbolts. After he defeated the Titans, he punished Atlas by making him carry the world on the western end of the universe. When Heracles went to the western most part of the world to pick the golden apples, as part of the twelve tasks given by Hera, he found Atlas there carrying the world. Only Atlas knew where the golden apples were. So he buried Atlas's load for a while and sent him forth to pick up the golden apples. When Atlas came back with the apples, he was not willing to carry the burden of the world anymore; however, Heracles tricked him into carrying the world again.

Atlas's other siblings Prometheus and Epimentheus sided with Zeus too; therefore, Zeus kept them near. When Zeus defeated the Titans and the Gigantes, he settled in Mount Olympus and formed the group of Twelve

A Roman-era statue of Atlas, who was condemned to bear the burden of the world as punishment. National Archaeological Museum of Naples.

Olympian gods together with his siblings and children. They shared the universe and began to rule from that location. Zeus took Prometheus near him because Prometheus not only did not object to him but also gave him ideas that helped him achieve victory. He was very cunning. He was able to deal with Zeus due to his intelligence and wit. But at times, he also drove Zeus crazy with his wiliness.

Zeus would join among the people sometimes and eat with them. On one occasion, it fell upon Prometheus to arrange the sharing of a sacrificed ox. Prometheus, who had always been a friend of human beings, resented Zeus somewhere deep inside for destroying his race. Therefore, he set the decent parts of the ox on one side, and the bones on the other side. He placed portions of paunch on top of the meat, and covered the bones with fatty portions. When he asked Zeus which part he would prefer, the god of gods reached for the nice-looking part. Zeus eventually realized that Prometheus was fooling him. He was outraged by his behavior and forbid fire to the beloved people of Prometheus out of vengeance. Thereupon, Prometheus hid some fire within a fennel stalk and brought it from Olympus back to the people. Let us learn from Hesiod what happened next:

Pandora

"Zeus who gathers the clouds said to him in anger:
Son of Iapetus, surpassing all in cunning,
You are glad that you have outwitted me and stolen fire
A great plague to you yourself and to men that shall be.
But I will give men as the price for fire an evil thing
In which they may all be glad of heart
While they embrace their own destruction."

So said the father of men and gods and laughed aloud. And he bade famous Hephaestus make haste:

"and mix earth with water and to put in it
the voice of and strength of human kind,
and fashion a sweet, lovely maiden-shape,
like to the immortal goddesses in face."

The order of Zeus was obeyed by Hephaestus immediately. This new creation was as beautiful as goddesses. Her face and her body were like those of a maiden's; youthful and proportionate. They put in her a spirit and life. Athena gave to her a girdle. The divine Charites put necklaces of gold upon her. The Horae crowned her head with spring flowers. They called this excessively beautiful first woman Pandora, meaning the gift of gods.

Plate image depicting an eagle eating the liver of Prometheus,
who was punished by Zeus. 550 BC, Vatican Museum.

Zeus commanded that this woman be sent to Epimetheus, who was not as
smart as his brother Prometheus. Prometheus admonished his brother not
to accept any gifts from the gods, knowing that his brother was not as
cunning as himself. He told him that the gift to be sent would become a
plague to the people. Epimetheus swore that he would not accept any
gifts. However, when the door was knocked and he saw an irresistibly
beautiful being outside, he forgot about all his promises and let her in. He
married this beautiful woman the next day.

Gods had also given Pandora a box. When Pandora opened the box, fears,
sorrows, illnesses and troubles sprang from it. They spread all over the
world before she was able to close the box. When the box was finally
closed, the only thing remaining inside was "hope" which made all
humanity chase after itself. Human beings, who lived without any trouble
unto that day, began to face great afflictions. Zeus's revenge against the
people proved to be harsh. The fact that this revenge was taken by way of
a woman made it even more painful.

Zeus now thought Prometheus needed to be punished. He ordered
Hephaestus to take him to the highest peak of the Caucasus Mountains
and shackle him there. He chained Prometheus to craggy rocks. Yet the

Embossment depicting Athena, Heracles and Atlas. 460 BC,
The Archaeological Museum of Olympia.

accounts were not settled for Zeus and he set an eagle on him. The eagle ate his liver every day. At night the liver would be regenerated and the eagle would start eating it again. This infliction went on and on under the burning sun.

While Prometheus served his punishment on the Caucasus Mountains, Zeus pursued new love affairs in Olympus. Around the same time, a prophecy was consuming Zeus internally. The prophecy was that a child to be born from a woman Zeus would marry was going to exceed him in power and overthrow him. Who was this child going to be born from? This could only be known by Prometheus who had foreseeing abilities. So, he forgave Prometheus and dispatched his son Heracles to bring him. Heracles slew the eagle which ate on Prometheus every day with its sharp beak. When Prometheus was elevated again to the echelon of gods, Zeus informed him of the threat facing him. This woman, the source of the threat, turned out to be Thetis, the daughter of Nereus, whom Zeus set his heart on and wanted to marry. However, fearing that the prophecy would come true, he had to bury his love in his heart. As a result, he had Thetis marry a mortal

Heracles rescuing Prometheus. Roman Period,
Aphrodisias Museum.

named Peleus. Even though Thetis resisted ardently not marrying the aged Peleus, she was not able to disobey the decision of the gods.

When Zeus decided to destroy the Iron Generation with a deluge, he told Deucalion, the son of foresighted Prometheus, to build a boat and to travel in this boat together with his wife Pyrrha. A vehement deluge began soon after, seizing and killing all the people. The boat on which Prometheus, his son, and wife were, tussled with the waters for nine consecutive days and nights and landed on top of Mount Parnassus. Having survived the disaster, Deucalion offered a sacrifice here to Zeus. This greatly contented Zeus and he in turn asked of Deucalion's wish via Hermes the messenger god. He wished the perished generation of humankind to be created again. Zeus said, "Throw behind you the bones of your mother." They were utterly confused by this remark. So, they went into the Temple of Themis and consulted with an oracle. The oracle also advised them to throw behind the bones of their mother, but Deucalion conceived that these were stones on the Mother Earth. Deucalion threw behind stones and they became men, and the stones that Pyrrha threw became women.

OLYMPUS

Zeus, who formed the third line of gods after Uranus and Cronus, began to dwell on Olympus, ruling the universe from there together with his siblings and children.

First denoted merely as a mountain, Olympus took on an ethereal connotation later. In a literal sense, it means a high mountain. Therefore, high mountains in Greece and Crete, as well as those in Anatolia such as Uludağ, were named Olympus. However, what actually comes to mind when one speaks of Olympus is the mountain lying between Macedonia and Thessaly with an altitude of 2,985 m. This is where people believed that gods resided in and ruled the world from. Zeus reigned from his throne in Olympus of countless peaks and observed what went on in the world. The palaces of the other gods were located downward from his. These palaces were made from bronze by Hephaestus, the blacksmith god.

Zeus would sit on his golden throne, while gods organized festivities before him, and thus they led a happy life. Their food and drink were not like those of the mortals. They consumed "ambrosia" and "nectar". Ambrosia, meaning 'immortal', was a type of honey made of multiple flower essences. Thus, the gods who fed on this would remain youthful and remain immortal. Goddess Hebe would serve the drinks inside golden cups. Afterwards, Zeus commissioned Ganymede (son of King Tros of Troy) to serve the drinks. Apollo and the Muses would jollify the festivities with their instruments and songs.

Gods would dress up like people, become angry and sad, and suffer like them. They would engage in fights and sometimes would be injured too. Even though their wounds hurt them, they would never kill them. Flowing in their bodies was not blood but a fluid called "ichor". On one occasion, Aphrodite and Ares had deep wounds and were writhing in pain, yet they did not die. The god Apollo applied a salve on their wounds and healed them.

There weren't always festivities in Olympus, at times there would be fights too. One time, Hephaestus the blacksmith god enraged Zeus and Zeus threw him down from Olympus and crippled him. On another occasion, some gods plotted a conspiracy against Zeus. This outraged Zeus and he punished Apollo and Poseidon by condemning them to work in the service of the king of Troy for one year.

Gods would never go against the orders of Zeus, the absolute ruler of Olympus. He was the head and king of gods and owner of the heavens. His order was law and his thunderbolts the symbol of his absolute dominion with which he would hit when angry. Although all the palaces of gods were in Olympus, Hades did not live in Olympus because he ruled the underworld. Besides Zeus, Hera, Hestia, Apollo, Artemis, Athena, Aphrodite, Poseidon, Ares, Hermes and Demeter, there were also secondary gods in Olympus. Of these deities, the

Greek	Latin	Representation of
Zeus	Jupiter	Air
Hera	Juno	Sky
Athena	Minerva	Lightning
Apollon	Apollo	Sun
Artemis	Diana	Moon
Hermes	Mercurius	Rain
Hephaestus	Vulcanus	Undergruond Fire
Hestia	Vesta	Hearth
Ares	Mars	Scythe, Storm
Aphrodite	Venus	Love
Demeter	Ceres	Earth
Poseidon	Neptunus	Sea

Names of Gods and Goddesses, What they Represent, and their Characteristics and Symbols

Muses, the divine Charites and the Horae would entertain the Olympians with their songs. The mother of the Horae, Themis, would sit near the throne of Zeus and spread justice. Her daughters Moirae helped their mother in spreading justice. The gods would sometimes be disguised as humans and go among them. As mentioned before, Zeus ruled the world from Olympus together with his siblings and children. Altogether, these gods were known as the twelve gods of Olympus.

Now the Greek and Latin names of these will be provided along with the natural powers they represented. And afterwards, we shall discuss the gods of Olympus one by one.

Characteristics	Symbols
Absolute power	Eagle, thunderbolt
Marriage	Peacock
Intelligence	Shield, olive branch
Fine arts, literature	Bow, lyre
Chastity	Stag, Crescent
Eloquence	Wings, wand with snakes
Industry	Hammer, anvil
Family values	Holy fire
War	Helmet, spear
Beauty	Dove
Abundance, fertility	Wheat ears, sickle
Rage	Trident spear

ZEUS = JUPITER

Zeus was the sixth and last child of Cronus and Rhea. Cronus would swallow his own newborns because he feared that his children would overthrow him as he did unto his father Uranus. In an effort to save her last child Zeus, Rhea gave birth in a cave in Crete and made her husband swallow a stone instead of Zeus.

Zeus was raised by a goat named Amalthea. Another rumor has it that Amalthea was in fact a nymph and she took the newborn Zeus to a cave on Mount Ida (Kazdağı) in western Anatolia and raised him with goat's milk. Again, fate played its part and when Zeus became an adult, he overthrew his father and preempted the throne. He saved his siblings, whom his father had swallowed earlier, by making his father drink a potion given by Metis the goddess of wisdom. Thus Zeus began to rule in Olympus together with his siblings.

Zeus combined all natural powers in himself related to the sky. Light, clouds, thunder, lightning; they were all embodied in Zeus. He is characterized in the Iliad as the one who collects clouds, who creates thunder and casts thunderbolts. It is this thundering god who established the dominion of gods for the third time, after Uranus and Cronus. The eagle was his sign of dominion to the eyes of people. On some occasions, he would display boundless tolerance for his wife Hera and on different occasions, he would confront her directly and disappoint her in her attempts.

Zeus married seven times according to Hesiod. First he married Metis, the Titan goddess of wisdom and this marriage produced Athena. Because it was prophesied that the children to be born from Metis would exceed their father Zeus in power, Zeus swallowed Metis during her labor and Athena was born from the head of her father, not from her mother. His second marriage was to goddess Themis who symbolized justice. From this marriage came forth the Horae who were named Eunomia, representing discipline, Dike, representing justice, and Eirene, representing peace. Also born were the Moirae who were goddesses of fate. Zeus's third wife was Dione of the Titans.

Statues from the western terrace of Mount Nemrut. Zeus is seen in the front, while Antiochus and Tyche are in the back.

Family of the Goddess	Name of the Goddess	Children
Daughter of Oceanus and Tethys Goddess of prudence	Metis	Athena
Natural organization of the seasons and art	Themis	The Horae, the Moirae
One of the three thousand Oceanids, born to Oceanus and Tethys *(Aphrodite was assumed to be born from sea foam, while according to Homer, she was the daughter of Dione.)*	Dione	Aphrodite
One of the three thousand Oceanids, born to Oceanus and Tethys. Goddess of harmony.	Eurynome	The Charites
Daughter of Uranus and Gaia Goddess of memory	Mnemosyne	The Muses
Daughter of Titan Coeus and Phoebe	Leto	Apollo, Artemis
Daughter Cronus and Rhea Goddess of fertility	Demeter	Persephone
Daughter of Cronus and Rhea, and sister of Zeus	Hera	Ares, Hebe, Eileithyia, Hephaestus

From her came forth Aphrodite. (There are also other versions of the birth of Aphrodite.) Oceanus and Tethys begat around three thousand daughters, and one of these was Eurynome. Zeus entered into his fourth marriage to her. In his Theogony, Hesiod tells of this marriage as follows:

"And Eurynome, the daughter of Ocean, beautiful in form, bare him three fair-cheeked Charites (Graces), Aglaea, and Euphrosyne, and lovely Thaleia."

Zeus's fifth wife was Mnemosyne. The Muses, fairies of art, were born from this marriage. His sixth marriage was to Leto. As is known, Apollo and Artemis were born from this marriage. Demeter was the seventh wife of Zeus. Persephone was born from this marriage. The last marriage of Zeus was to Hera. Hera gave birth to Hebe, Ares and Eileithyia in this marriage. As is known, Ares became the god of war.

Family of the mortal woman (Zeus united in love with many immortal women and had many children with them as well)	Name of the mortal woman	Children
Wife of King Amphitryon	Alcmene	Heracles
Daughter of the Theban King Nycteus	Antiope	Amphion, Zethus
Daughter of the Arcadian King Lycion	Callisto	Arcas
Daughter of King Acrisius of Argos	Danae	Perseus
Daughter of the river god Asopus	Aegina	Aeacus
One of the seven Peliades, who were daughters of Atlas and Pleione	Electra	Dardanos,Iasion, Harmonia
Daughter of the Phoenician King Agenor	Europa	Minos, Sarpedon, Rhadamanthys
Daughter of King Inachus of Argos	Io	Epaphos
Lycian daughter of Bellerophontes	Laodameia	Sarpedon
Daughter of the Aetolian king Thestius	Leda	Helen, the Dioscuri
One of the seven Pleiades born to Atlas and Pleione	Maia	Hermes
A Lydian woman	Pluto	Tantalus
Daughter of the Lydian king Tantalus, who was the son of Zeus and Pluto	Niobe	Argus, Pelasgus
Daughter of the Theban King Cadmus and Harmonia	Semele	Dionysus
Daughter of Atlas and Pleione	Taygete	Lacedaemon

Furthermore, his union with the titan Atlas's daughter, Maia on Mount Kellene of Arcadia, produced Hermes, and his union with Semele, the daughter of Cadmos, produced Dionysus. Again, Zeus's union with Asteria, the daughter of titan Coeus, produced the goddess Hecate.

Apart from these marriages, Zeus had secret love affairs as well. He begat many children from these love affairs, which he engaged in unsuspected by his wife Hera. These relationships will now be discussed briefly. Zeus immensely admired Alcmene, the beautiful and virtuous wife of Amphitryon. While Amphitryon was on his way back from a victorious battle, Zeus forestalled by disguising himself as him and went to Alcmene's bed. After a few hours, the real husband came and lay with his wife. Alcmene gave birth to twins named Heracles and Iphicles after these intercourses. Of these twins, Heracles is assumed to

Temple of Zeus at Euromos, near Milas. Roman Period.

be the son of Zeus. Hera spent her life striving to take revenge from Heracles who was born from this affair. Consequently, Heracles engaged in chivalrous acts and thus made for himself a name.

One day by the sea, Zeus saw beautiful Europa, the daughter of the Phoenician King Agenor, admired her greatly and began to desire her. But how was he to come together with this beautiful girl without letting his jealous wife Hera know? He immediately thought of an idea; he disguised himself as a bull and went to the lawn on which the girl was playing with her friends. Beautiful Europa saw this cute bull

grazing near them and could not help but fondle it. In his most adorable manner, the bull let her caress him and rolled on the ground. Europa suggested to her friends that they ride on the bull and take a stroll. They all accepted this suggestion. Europa mounted and sat on the broad back of the bull. While the others were still setting about to mount on it, the seemingly docile bull began to run all of a sudden and abducted the beautiful girl. Europa's friends watched in disbelief as the bull cut across the sea and ran as if travelling on a level plain.

At last, the bull stopped on the island of Crete, put the beautiful girl down underneath the shadow of a large plane tree and appeared as a god again. Under the dark and cool shadow of the tree, he ravished this beautiful girl whom he admired so much. Therefore, King Minos of Crete came into the world from this union.

Zeus admired Io, the daughter of King Inachus of Argos. Io was a nun at the Temple of Hera in the city of Argos. Zeus seduced Io by disguising himself as a cloud. Zeus then transformed the girl into a cow to save her from Hera who discovered this relationship. Hera asked Zeus to give the cow to her as a gift, and Zeus could not decline this wish and gave her the cow. Hera actually saw through the scheme and he put her under the watch of Argus, a hundred-eyed monster. Zeus charged Hermes with rescuing his lover. Hermes went near the monster with his magic wand and pipe. He made the monster sleep by telling it stories and playing his pipe, and killed it afterwards. Hera took the eyes of the monster and placed them into the tails of her sacred pet peacock. Meanwhile, the cow escaped and Hera dispatched a gadfly to follow her. The cow ran and the gadfly chased. Thus the cow passed the seas and territories. The first sea that Io passed is known as Ionia, and the first strait she passed is known as the Bosphorus meaning the "passage of cow". At last, Io managed to stop by the Nile, where Zeus restored her to human form again. There, she gave birth to a child named Epaphus.

Regardless the jealousies of his wife Hera, Zeus the god of gods continued his love affairs. Next, he fell in love with Danae, the daughter of King Acrisius of Argos. This king had no sons and he had learnt from the oracles that the child to be born from his daughter would overthrow him. Therefore, he enclosed his daughter within a chamber with bronze walls. In the form of a golden rain drop, Zeus seeped through an opening on the ceiling of the chamber and fell over the lap of the girl. Famous Perseus was born from this union.

One day in his palace in Olympus, Zeus was sitting at a distant place from his wife and thinking of something entertaining to do. During this time, he admired Leda the daughter of the king of Aetolia and wife of King Tyndareus of Sparta. While Leda was taking a bath in the lake, Zeus disguised himself as a swan and approached her.

On the same day, Leda united with her husband Tyndareus. Two embryos came into being after this union. Both of the embryos

Temple of Zeus, Aizanoi. Pseudodipteros, 8 x 15 columns, Ionic order.
Reign of Hadrian AD 117 - 138.

developed into twins. Helen and Castor were assumed to be from Zeus, Clytemnestra and Polydeuces were assumed to be from Leda's husband.

Zeus the god of gods, who was a true rascal, was never satiated when it came to beautiful women. Despite his fear, he could not help but cheat on his wife Hera with every woman he admired. One day, he fell in love with Antiope, the beautiful daughter of King Nycteus of Thebes. He disguised himself as a satyr and ravished her. The King soon found out that his daughter was pregnant and he sent his daughter out from his country without knowing whom she conceived from. Zeus begat two children from Antiope named Zethus and Amphion. The children were raised in the mountains by shepherds. Later, they both became rulers in the city of Thebes. Zeus was later enamored of Aegina, the daughter of Asopus the river god. Aegina was Antiope's sister. Disguised as an eagle and fire, Zeus kidnapped his sweetheart to the island of Oenone and ravished her there. Here, Aegina brought forth Aeacus from Zeus.

Another love affair Zeus engaged in was with Callisto, the daughter of the Arcadian king Lycaon. This beautiful girl was Artemis's friend and had promised her that she would remain immaculate and pure. But she too was tempted and impregnated by Zeus. Artemis realized that Callisto was defiled and became very mad at her. The girl gave birth to a child named Arcas. Zeus transformed her into a bear to save her from the wrath of Artemis. Years later, while Arcas was hunting in the woods, his mother came across him in the form of a bear. Arcas was about to trap her unknowingly but Zeus could not wait any longer and hoisted his lover into the heavens and transformed her into the constellation known as the "Great Bear" and his son into the one known as the "Little Bear".

Zeus's Temples and Depictions

Zeus was illustrated as a mature man, with his symbolic eagle, holding a thunderbolt in his right hand, and a wand in his left hand. He was mostly shown while sitting on his throne. The sculptures of him generally depict him with thick, wavy hair, a broad forehead, an impressive stern-looking face surrounded by a beard. Very rarely is he seen naked except for his earlier depictions. In his nude depictions, he has a cloak leaving his right arm and chest open. His sacred animal was the eagle and his sacred plant was the oak. His oracle was in

Dodona, which was located in Northern Greece known as the land of oak trees, near the Albanian border. For this reason, Zeus sometimes wore a wreath of oak leaves.

One of the most important temples for Zeus is the temple in the city of Olympia to the west of the Peloponnese. This is where his cult statue was made from gold and ivory, by the famous sculptor Phidias around 435 BC. This Doric temple with 6 x 13 columns dates to the 5th century BC. The Temple of Olympian Zeus (Olympeion) in Athens, which is in the Corinthian style, dates to the 2nd century BC. The temple, where 15 columns remain standing, became identified with the city of Athens. The games and competitions held every year at the Olympeion in the name of Zeus turned into the Olympic games of this time. The Temple of Zeus at Akragas, Italy, is the most spectacular one among the Doric temples which remain standing today. The temple measures 53 x 110 m and dates to the 5th century BC.

Many spectacular temples were erected for Zeus in many antique cities in Anatolia. Among these, the most famous and the ones that are still standing are the Temple of Zeus at Uzuncaburç dating to the Hellenistic Period, and the Temple of Zeus at Euromos near Milas dating to the Roman age, as well as the Temple of Zeus at Aizanoi near Çavdarhisar. The Temple of Zeus at Uzuncaburç has 6 x 12 columns and is the oldest known temple in the Corinthian style. The 3rd century BC temple has an extraordinary look with its columns that are intact. The Temple of Zeus at Euromos, which has 6 x 11 columns, is in the Corinthian style and is picturesque, appearing among olive trees. The Temple of Zeus in Aizanoi from the Roman Period is one of those rare temples that protected its original form to this date. There are 8 columns on the short sides of the marble temple and 15 columns on the long sides of it, which remain standing today. Apart from these temples that reached to this date intact, there are other temples dedicated to Zeus in many antique cities. In the Caria region of Anatolia, Zeus was worshipped as Zeus Stratios and a spectacular temple was erected for him in Labranda. As Phidias, other artists too illustrated Zeus on a throne. His symbol, an eagle, was sometimes depicted near his throne, sometimes at the tip of his wand and sometimes on top of his hands. The 5th century BC bronze sculpture of him at the National Museum of Athens is one of the most splendid sculptures of him. At a temple on the island of Corfu, Zeus is illustrated on the pediment while fighting against the giants. Zeus

Statue of Zeus, the chief god, found in Aydın. Hellenistic Period.
İstanbul Archaeology Museums.

reliefs can be seen on the pediments of the temple in Selinus, Bologna
and of many others. There are also beautiful samples from the Roman
Period depicting Zeus, or Jupiter, as known in Latin. The most
beautiful examples of these are the temple in Capitolium and the
temples of Jupiter Stator and Jupiter Victor at the foot of the Palatine
Hill. Various sculptures, busts and head statues of Zeus have been
obtained and he has been among the inevitable subjects for the arts
of painting and sculpture to this day. The head statue of Zeus from the
2nd century BC at the Bergama (Pergamum) Museum and the one that

Statue of Zeus found in Perge. 2ⁿᵈ century AD, Antalya Museum.

was found in Troy and is exhibited at the İstanbul Archaeology Museum today, depict him exquisitely. His thick hair and beard, and the poignant look in his eyes would suit those of a chief god. The head statue of Zeus, which was excavated in the antique city of Sagalassos and is exhibited at the Burdur Museum, is one of these typical examples. It is also possible to see many beautiful sculptures of Zeus today at the National Museum of Athens, Louvre Museum, British Museum, among others including the ones in Turkey such as İstanbul Archaeology Museum, Antalya Museum and the Museum of Anatolian Civilizations in Ankara.

HERA ⋈ JUNO

Hera, who was the daughter of Cronus and Rhea, was swallowed by her father. Zeus saved her from the stomach of Cronus and married her. Zeus appeared to Hera in the form of a bird chilled by the cold weather on a winter day, and Hera held the chilled bird to her bosom. However, Zeus restored to his original self and attempted to ravish her. Hera resisted but she accepted on condition that they married. According to the legend, the wedding celebration of Zeus and Hera took place at the Garden of the Hesperides in the west. From this marriage between Zeus and Hera came forth Ares, Hephaestus, Eileithyia and Hebe. A typical Greek goddess, Hera was ill-tempered, quarrelsome, covetous and resentful. Therefore she appears as an obnoxious goddess. She always wanted to settle matters by crafty means; therefore, Zeus addresses her as the "trickster" in the Iliad.

Goddess Hera was unable to do anything against her rascal husband Zeus, so she would harm the women he united in love with and the children born from these unions. There was nobody fit to hold a candle to Hera in terms of craftiness. All her life, Hera endeavored to punish Heracles, who was born from a love affair of Zeus. Zeus would sometimes lose his patience with Hera for the things she did to Heracles and punish her by hanging her upside down, tying anvils on to her feet and golden chains on to her hands.

However, Hera would not come around. She even wanted the destruction and vanishment of Troy just because a Trojan refused to give the golden apple to her. She supported the Achaeans throughout the war. In fact, when the Trojans were driving back the Achaeans in one instance, Hera came down from Olympus hastily, approached Zeus who was watching the war on Mount Ida and seduced him. When Zeus fell asleep, she helped the Achaeans together with other deities. Zeus became outraged when he woke and saw what happened.

"I see, Hera," said he,
"you mischief-making trickster,
That your cunning has stayed Hector from fighting,
And has caused the rout of his host.

Statue of Hera Ephesia found in Sagalassos.
The first half of the 2nd century AD Roman Period. Burdur Museum.

I am in half a mind to thrash you,
In which case you will be the first to reap the fruits of your scurvy
knavery.
Do you not remember how once upon a time I had you hanged?"

Hera was the goddess of family ties and births. Even though she was upset by the affairs of Zeus, she never cheated on him. She possessed a reserved and mature beauty. She would go to the spring of Kanathos every year, where she took a bath and regained her virginity and beauty from the enchanted waters.

She was the most beautiful woman of Olympus after Aphrodite. Hence, many confessed their love to her yet she never felt any interest in them. Ixion, for example, was the major one among those who courted her. Everybody on earth hated Ixion because he had his father-in-law burnt alive; however, Zeus had forgiven him and even accepted him to Olympus. There, Ixion plagued Hera, who in turn complained about him to Zeus. He was punished by being dumped into hell. Hera was the inherent protector of Achilles. Because she raised Achilles's mother Thetis.

Ravage winds that were trapped in the caves of Thrace and Sicily were at her disposal. When she wanted to punish somebody, she would give an order to Aeolus, the guardian of the winds, have him release the winds, and the winds would wreck the ships in the sea, tear down homes or slam trees.

Since Hera was the protector of marriage and maternity, she is described as a plump young woman. Magnificent and solemn, she has a demure face and thoughtful eyes. She wears a garment that covers her body. In statues, she is mostly illustrated as sitting on a high throne. She holds a wand with a cuckoo at its tip in one hand. This bird was the symbol of her marriage to Zeus. The peacock was her sacred animal and pomegranate was her sacred plant. Her face is depicted as beautiful. Her eyes are large and beautiful; her hair is rendered thick and as if bursting out of her tiara. A veil is attached to the back of her head, reminiscent of a bridal veil.

Hera watched over births with her daughter Eileithyia and the most well-known temple of her is Heraion of Samos. Her statue, which was found here and dates to 405 BC, is exhibited at the Louvre Museum today. The Temple of Hera in Olympia from the 6th century BC presents a splendid view with its columns that remain to be standing and the trees at the background. Apart from this one, the Temple of Hera from the

Embossment of Hera, Delphi Museum.

5th century BC, which is located in Selinus in Sicily, is still erect with its entire splendor. There are two temples for Hera dating to 460 and 430 BC in Paestum, which was established as a Greek colony to the south of Napoli in Italy. These are Doric in style. There is another temple for Hera 6 km. from Paestum at the mouth of the river Sele, which dates to around 520 BC. Akragas which was also established as a Greek colony on the southern coast of Sicily (a place with increasing wealth and power at the time) is home to an extremely well-preserved temple for Hera (Juno) located in the valley of gods. The Temple of Hera, which dates to 450 BC and was built in the Doric style, deserves a visit too.

The cult of Hera, or Iuno (Juno) as known in Latin, became widespread in Greece and Rome. Goddess Hera, who was nagging, jealous, grumpy, stubborn and a trickster, contrasts the stereotype of an amiable Anatolian personality, which accounts for her bad reputation in Anatolia.

POSEIDON ᴴ NEPTUNUS

When the Universe was divided among the gods, the seas were taken by Poseidon who is called Neptunus in Latin. Thus he became the sole ruler of the seas, coasts and islands. Poseidon means the "ruler of the sea". It is often cited in legends as the "earth-shaking god". Poseidon is the son of Cronus and Rhea and brother of Zeus. He had an undying resentment against Zeus, whom he sometimes challenged but had to give in each time in the face of Zeus's power. He shook the earth with the help of his trident fishing spear, frothed the sea but would remain weak compared to the thunderbolts of Zeus.

Poseidon married Amphitrite, who was one of the fifty daughters born from the union of Doris (Oceanus's daughter) and Nereus. They lived in their golden palace on the sea between Tenedos and Imbros (respectively Bozcaada and Gökçeada in Turkish). There were many water deities at the disposal of Poseidon. Daughters of Nereus were among these. Leading among them were Achilles's mother Thetis and Amphitrite. Poseidon's marriage to Amphitrite produced Triton who would raise or calm the waves. He too was at the disposal of Poseidon. Following them in rank were the Nymphs, who were depicted as nubile maidens and represented the uplifting power of water. Apart from these, Poseidon also begat notorious giant sons from other women. His marriage to Gaia brought forth Antaeus. Heracles defeated this giant and secured the roads. Form the union of Poseidon with a nymph named Thoosa came forth Polyphemus who was a Cyclopes. When Polyphemus ate Odysseus's men in a cave, Odysseus blinded him by sticking a hot olive branch into his eye. Poseidon exacted revenge on Odysseus for his son by driving him from one sea to another for years. Poseidon's union with Aethra, daughter of King Pittheus of Troezen, brought forth Theseus. Poseidon would unleash sea monsters upon those whom he wanted to punish. This is how he punished King Laomedon of Troy who failed to pay Poseidon and Apollo their wages for building the walls of Troy as Zeus condemned them to do. A Trojan priest who declared that the Trojan horse was a trick, Laocoon was suffocated together with his sons by the snakes of Poseidon.

Bronze statue of Poseidon, which was taken out of the sea off the coast of Artemision. 460 BC.

This scene of suffocation became a source of inspiration for sculptors, generating a visually appealing sculpture art. Poseidon admired Demeter. He wanted to seduce her but was rejected by her. Demeter disguised herself as a horse to escape him but Poseidon disguised himself as a horse too and ravished her. It is also told that he made love to the gorgon Medusa on the grass. Poseidon rode on his chariot pulled by four purebred horses with golden mane. The waves would calm down where his chariot passed and all sea animals would swim by his chariot. When he was mad, boisterous waves would hit the coasts, spreading their white foams around. He did not only rule the seas, he could shatter the coasts if he saw fit.

There are various magnificent marble and bronze sculptures of Poseidon at museums. The bronze Poseidon sculpture at Louvre is very impressive and dates to the 2nd century BC. The bronze sculpture of Poseidon at the National Museum of Athens, dating to 460 BC, is also marvelous. There are replicas of this bronze sculpture in other museums. The Madrid, Louvre and Vatican museums are also home to sculptures of Poseidon. A marble sculpture of Poseidon found on the island of Melos, which dates to 130 BC, is also at the National Museum of Athens. In addition to the temples devoted to Poseidon in Greece, which date to 5th century BC, the ones devoted to Neptune in Italy are also very enchanting. Not many temples can be spoken of in his name in Anatolia since he did not have much activity there.

Turkish museums have many sculptures of Poseidon as well, in which he quite resembles Zeus. A remarkable example is a statue of Poseidon together with Demeter from the 2nd century BC, which was found at the agora of İzmir and is exhibited in the Museum of İzmir today.

He is depicted as broad shouldered and with his long curly hair flowing down on his shoulders, either naked or with clothes, but always with his trident fishing spear in his hand. He is sometimes illustrated as stepping on a rock or the back of a dolphin. Tuna fish, dolphins, horses and bulls were animals that were dedicated to him. His wife Amphitrite is depicted with her wet hair gathered in a net, accompanied by dolphins, tritons and oysters. Poseidon is also known as Neptune in Latin. He is also seen on the altar reliefs of Pergamum while fighting against the Giants on his chariot drawn by four horses on the mosaics.

The cult of Poseidon was acclaimed in places such as Delphi,

Marble statues of Poseidon and Demeter, found and still standing in the Agora of İzmir. 2ⁿᵈ century AD. İzmir Archaeological Museum.

Thessaly, Athens, Corinth and Delos. There is a 5th century BC. Doric temple dedicated to him on Cape Sounion located to the south of Athens in Greece on a mountainous area overlooking the sea, which is looked up to admiringly by the passing ships.

Paestum was one of the most beautiful and developed cities established by the Hellenic tribes in Southern Italy, which is known as Magna Graecia today. Many temples in this area survived intact to this date. The Temple of Poseidon from the 5th century BC, is also remarkable with its spectacular outlook.

DEMETER ᴴ CERES

Demeter, who was the daughter of Cronus and Rhea, was the goddess of earth and fertility of the earth. Demeter's daughter Persephone, whom Homer refers to as having beautiful hair, was abducted by Hades the god of the underworld while picking flowers in the meadow. Demeter scoured the globe for her daughter, whom she bore from Zeus, and was unable to find her anywhere. When she was about to abandon hope, Helios the god of Sun told her the whereabouts of her daughter.

So Demeter went to Zeus and asked for his help to rescue her daughter. Hades refused to give her daughter back, so Demeter left Olympus bitter and twisted, disguised as a mortal old woman and began to roam various cities. When she arrived at a town named Eleusis, she stopped by the house of King Celeus and offered to the wife of the king, Metaneira, that she would nurse her son. The queen accepted the offer and gave his son Demophon to Demeter to be raised by her. Demeter loved the child and fed him with the food of gods and wished to immortalize him by holding him to fire. The behaviors of this old woman, though, raised doubts in the mind of the queen, and one day she actually caught her while holding the child to fire. Tremendously petrified, the queen scolded Demeter. After this, Demeter had to explain to the queen that he was actually going to become immortal if it weren't for her, and she transformed into a goddess again. Later the king and the queen erected a temple in Eleusis and dedicated it to Demeter, thus trying to propitiate to her.

Because Demeter fell out with nature in the absence of her daughter, she ceased the fertility of the earth and a drought prevailed. Thereupon, Zeus had to reconcile Demeter and Hades, and they agreed that the child would spend the half of the year with her mother and the rest with her husband in the land of the dead. Each time Persephone came out of the ground to be with her mother, the flowers blossomed, and the spring came. Her return to the underworld symbolized winter.

Statue of Demeter. 340-330 BC. It was taken out of Turkey in 1857 and is exhibited at the British Museum.

Bronze statue of Demeter from around 400 BC. İzmir Museum.

Poseidon lost his heart to this blonde goddess, but Demeter refused his love. Still, reportedly, Poseidon disguised himself into various appearances and seduced Demeter. It is known that Zeus also fell in love with this beautiful goddess and had his daughter Persephone (Kore) by her. There is a beautiful sculpture of Persephone (Kore) from the 5th century BC, and many head statues of her at the Acropolis Museum in Athens. Demeter fell in love with Iasion, a mortal, and lay with him in a thrice-ploughed field. She bore Plutus from this union. Plutus was the personification of wealth and fertility. When he declared that he was not going to give wealth to the immoral and graceless, Zeus blinded him and distributed his wealth among the public.

In her sculptures, Demeter is shown as a beautiful woman with languid eyes and blonde hair flowing down on her shoulders. A wreath of wheat ears decorates her hair. A bust of Demeter, which was taken out of the sea by sponge hunters in Bodrum, can be seen at the

Statue of Demeter from around 530-520 BC.

İzmir Museum today. There is another sculpture of her at the same museum, depicting her together with Poseidon. Demeter holds a wheat ear in her right hand, and a burning torch in her left hand. She was sometimes shown with a wand or a sickle in her hand. Opium poppy was her sacred flower. She would also wear wreaths made of myrtle or narcissus. The magnificent sculpture of Demeter found in Knidos and dating to 340 BC can be seen at the British Museum today. There is a temple dedicated to Demeter in Eleusis in Greece, to the west of Athens. Most of the Demeter temples in Greece were built on open field, outside the city walls. There were holy sites for Demeter in the antique cities of Pergamum and Priene. She was referred to as Ceres in Rome. There is another temple for Demeter in the antique city of Akragas, which is located on the Island of Sicily. The group of sculptures illustrating the threesome of Kore, Demeter and Hebe, which was discovered at the acropolis of Athens and can be seen at the British Museum today, dates to 432 BC.

Aphrodite means sea foam in Greek. The goddess of love and beauty, Aphrodite was born from sea foam and was flirtatious and enticing as such. As told in Hesiod's Theogony, Aphrodite, who came about from the seeds of Uranus that poured into the sea, was drifted by waves to the Island of Cyprus in an oyster shell. Aphrodite was thus born out of the blue waters of the Mediterranean. This child of the Mediterranean soon took her place in Greece as a goddess. According to Homer, on the other hand, Aphrodite was born from Dione, the daughter of Zeus and Oceanus.

The goddess of love was also recognized by different names such as Ishtar by the Assyrians and Astarte by the Phoenicians. This gorgeous being took her part in Olympus as a goddess symbolizing beauty, grace and fertility, surrounded by the Charites and Horae.

Aphrodite enlivened nature which spread out love to hearts. It was accepted that her helping hand influenced every beauty in blooming nature. And her son Eros, who shot arrows of love into hearts and whom she bore from Hermes, would never leave her side.

Aphrodite lay with Ares the god of war, and from this union came forth Phobos (fear), Deimos (dread) and Harmonia (harmony). Aphrodite also lay with Adonis, the son of the King of Cyprus. The King had a strikingly beautiful daughter named Myrrha, and her mother claimed that she was more beautiful than Aphrodite. In response, Aphrodite cursed Myrrha by making her fall in love with her own father and sleep with him. When he discovered the situation, the King wanted to kill his daughter but the gods spared her by transforming her into a myrtle tree. Thus Adonis was arisen from this myrtle tree. Nymphs, the fairies of nature, looked after the newborn, who eventually became a handsome young man. One fine day, Eros erroneously shot his mother Aphrodite with the arrow of love and the arrow made her fall in love with Adonis desperately. However, their love did not last very long because Adonis was killed by a boar while hunting. Aphrodite lay with Hermes and this union produced the androgynous Hermaphroditus. One day, Hermaphroditus wanted to take a bath in the Bardakçı Cove across from Bodrum. A girl named Salmacis

Aphrodite of Milos from the 2ⁿᵈ century BC.

saw him there and was struck by him. She jumped into the water and embraced this young man. When she was refused by him, she pleaded with the gods and wished not be parted with him. Her wish was granted and she became a part of him: Hermaphroditus was transformed into an androgynous being now. Aphrodite's union with Dionysus brought forth Priapus, who was a bizarre being with his huge male genital.

Aphrodite, who was chosen as the most beautiful goddess on Mount Ida by Paris, was eventually given in marriage to the lame god Hephaestus. Aphrodite did not love her husband, the lame god of blacksmiths. The account of her infidelity to her husband with Ares and their captivation by Hephaestus in a golden net is told in Homer's Odyssey. She also lay with Anchises of Dardania, from the royal lineage of Troy, and gave birth to the famed Aeneas. After the devastation of Troy, Aeneas was the one who brought the survivors to Rome.

Beautiful, flirtatious and enticing as she was, the anger, resentment and vengeance of the goddess was much dreaded as well. When they stirred her anger, she would afflict the women of Lemnos with such odor that their husbands would no longer approach their wives. In some instances, the goddess would plague the women arousing her anger with such lust that they would feel compelled to lie with whomever comes along. This would continue until her anger subsided.

Aphrodite was surrounded by the Charites, who symbolized beauty, grace and fertility, namely whatever appealed to the eye. Charis means beauty and glamour. The Charites were goddesses which spread joy and happiness to the hearts of gods and people. These goddesses were born from Eurynome the goddess of harmony, who was the daughter of Zeus and Oceanus. They were also known as the Three Graces and were named Aglaea, Euphrosyne and Thalia. Other deities around Aphrodite were the Horae, and the Hymenaeuses who would lead wedding processions.

Praxiteles the sculptor created two statues of Aphrodite around 350 BC. One of them is a nude depiction, while the other is clothed.

The nude one was taken by the city of Knidos on the coast of the Mediterranean and erected at the town center. Antique authors wrote about sailors setting sale to the Anatolian coasts to see this most beautiful statue of the world. When the people of Knidos went into great

Roman-era copy of the Aphrodite of Arles by Praxiteles.

Roman-era copy of the Aphrodite of Genetrix from 430-400 BC. Louvre Museum.

debt during the 1st century BC, Nicomedes II claimed this statue in return for his loan; however, people of Knidos paid every penny of their debt but did not give their sculpture. Ancient historians wrote that this sculpture was brought to the Palace of Lausus in Constantinople during Byzantine times and was consumed in flames when the palace burnt. Depicting a nude goddess for the first time, Praxiteles showed in this sculpture all the beauty, charm and curves of womanhood. The clothed

Aphrodite of Knidos. The terracotta figurine is the Roman-era copy of the 4ᵗʰ century-BC work. Çanakkale Museum.

version of the Aphrodite sculpture was taken by the people of Cos (Island of İstanköy) and erected in their city. Praxiteles also cast a sculpture of Aphrodite in half-clothed form, which is known as the Aphrodite of Arles. In a divine beauty contest judged by Paris, in which Aphrodite competed against Athena and Hera to win the golden apple, Aphrodite offered to give Paris the most beautiful woman on earth, Helen, and thus won the contest. She kept her promise by having beautiful Helen enamored of Paris. Aphrodite was accepted as goddess of love in Greece and Rome; whereas in Anatolia, she was a goddess symbolizing fertility. In Aphrodisias, where she was the chief deity, Aphrodite did not only symbolize beauty; her multiple-breasted form was the symbol of fertility. She came to be identified with Cybele, the fertility goddess of Anatolia. A marvelous temple was built for Aphrodite in Aphrodisias. This temple is still standing today with 14 columns, arousing admiration in onlookers. Constructed in the Late Hellenistic period, the temple was surrounded by a temenos during the reign of Hadrianus (AD 117-138). The tetrapylon, which was built on the path leading to the temple, has been restored and re-erected today, setting an impressive display. Many head statues of Aphrodite were found during the excavations of Aphrodisias (which were also attended by the author of this book). These head statues, excelling one another in beauty, can be seen today at the Aphrodisias Museum today.

Artistic representations of Aphrodite usually render her as coming out of a sea shell. With her beautiful hair, innocent face and proportionate body, she became a source of inspiration to sculptors in depicting an ideal woman body. The Birth of Venus is a painting by Sandro Botticelli that features Aphrodite. The source text of this art work is thought to have been written by the Latin poet Ovid.

Plants and fruits devoted to her were myrtle tree, opium poppy, apple, pomegranate, and rose. Her sacred birds were sparrow and pigeon. Animals devoted to her were goat, oyster, dolphin and tortoise. She was revered as Venus in Rome. Early on in the Archaic art, Aphrodite was depicted as fully clothed, sometimes seated but mostly standing. From the 5th century BC onwards, some parts of her body began to be revealed. During the Hellenistic period, when nudity predominated, she was mostly shown as naked while stepping out of sea or bath.

Aphrodite of Alcamenes, which dates to the 5th century BC and is in the Louvre Museum today, shows her with a light tulle on her body. The Roman-era copy of "Aphrodite Genetrix" sculptured by Callimachus around the 5th century BC is in the Louvre Museum, while the Roman copies of the Aphrodite of Knidos, created by Praxiteles as nude, can be seen in the Vatican and many other museums. Half-clothed Aphrodite by Praxiteles, which is presently at the Louvre Museum, is a Roman copy of Aphrodite of Arles.

The most famous of the sculptures recovered to date is the half-naked Aphrodite created by Lysippos on the Island of Melos. Discovered among

Statue of Venus while taking a bath, by Doidalses of Bithynia.
Roman-era marble copy of the original bronze statue from
the 3rd century BC.

theatre ruins on Melos, the 2nd century-BC, sculpture is at the Louvre Museum today. This is why half-clothed sculptures of Aphrodite are known as Aphrodite of Melos.

Medici Venus by Kleomenes, dating to the 1st century BC, was found in Florence and is another half-nude Roman copy. There is also the Capuan Venus from the 4th century at the Therme Museum in Rome, as well as a Roman copy of Aphrodite of Knidos created by Praxiteles in 350 BC, which is in the Vatican Museum.

A Roman copy of the Capitoline Venus dating to 320 BC and illustrating Aphrodite as coming out of bath, is in the Capitoline Museums today.

There are many sculptures of Aphrodite in Turkish Museums too. The terracotta Aphrodite of Knidos in the Çanakkale Museum is one of them. Sculptures of Aphrodite can also be seen in museums such as İstanbul Archaeology, Antalya, Aphrodisias and İzmir.

ATHENA
PERGE [3.79]
2 nd Cent. A.D.

After Zeus acquired dominion in Olympus, he united with Metis the goddess of prudence and thought. The child to be born from this union was said to overthrow Zeus. Just when Metis was about to deliver her baby, Zeus swallowed it. Before long, however, he began suffering an intense headache. To appease this unbearable headache, he ordered Hephaestus the blacksmith god to cleave his head with an axe. Fulfilling Zeus's order, Hephaestus did so, and Athena sprang out of the cleavage in his head, well equipped with arms.

She took her place in Olympus along with the other deities. Athena, who was the personification of subtle mind, craftiness and thinking, was the contrast of Ares in Olympus, as the goddess of rightful war. And, because Zeus favored Athena the most among his children, he gave his shield and flaming thunderbolt to her only.

Not even the war god Ares knew war tricks as well as she did. She also invented many tools and musical instruments and taught people how to use them. It was announced that the city of Athens was going to be given to a deity who would be most beneficial. A competition was launched for this purpose, whereby Poseidon spurted sea water from the ground and Athena planted an olive tree. The referees thought Athena's deed was more beneficial and thus left the patronage of Athens to her.

This came as no surprise because Athena, as the goddess of prudence, was quick to reckon a more beneficial way due to her ingenuity. As a divine maiden, she was also the impersonation of virtue. Homer refers to her as the grey-eyed Pallas. Her being named as Pallas could have been because she killed the giant named Pallas during the war against the giants. Athena stripped off the skin of the giant and made herself an aegis from it. The sculpture of Pallas Athena was assumed to have magical attributions and was named Palladium.

Athena was also called by many names other than Pallas. For example, Promachus, meaning the one who fights on the front line; Polias, due to her guardianship of cities, Parthenos, due to her embodiment of virginhood, and Pronoea, as the symbol of wisdom, were among these

Statue of Athena found in Perge. Antalya Museum.

names. Her depiction in the Iliad is more like a war goddess. On every occasion, she protects the Achaeans and plots schemes against the Trojans. It is not clear whether this bias was because she was the guardian goddess of the city of Athens, or due to a feminine grudge against Paris of Troy for not choosing her as the most beautiful among the goddess.

Homer's Iliad portrays her as an obnoxious, trickster and violent war goddess, while she is seen more as an amiable goddess in the Odyssey, symbolizing prudence and knowledge.

Emulously protecting her virginity, Athena was at the same time very fond of her beauty. One day, she saw her reflection in the water while playing the pipe, supposedly her own invention, and realized how ugly this rendered her and threw it away and walked away. Marsyas, who later found this pipe and became adept at playing it, was to suffer many incidents. Athena was also the inventor of the war chariot drawn by four horses and the mastermind in the building of the ship of Argo.

Athena contested against Poseidon the god. She also competed with a mortal named Arachne, who was famous for her excellence in weaving and was from the town of Colophon near Ephesus (Ephesos).

Athena is generally seen in her statues as armed from top to toe. She is seen as holding her shield in one hand and a spear in her other hand, while wearing a headpiece. Her shield and her breastplate bear the head of Medusa on them. Some of her statues depict her as the embodiment of virgin beauty; serious, prudent and unarmed.

At the Temple of Parthenon, which was dedicated to Athena, there was a sculpture of the goddess created by Phidias at a height of 9 meters from gold-plated ivory. In front of the same temple, the bronze statue depicting her as the "frontline fighter" was also cast by Phidias. Unfortunately, these exquisite works of art from the Antiquity have disappeared now, but their Roman copies at the Athens Museum can give an idea. There are replicas of originals such as of Athena Medici and Athena of Velletri dating approximately to 440-430 BC in Paris; Athena Albani dating approximately to 440 BC in the Villa Albani in Rome; Athena Giustiniani dating to 400 BC's in the Vatican Museum, Ince Athena dating around to 400 BC in Liverpool, and Athena Hope dating to late 5th century BC in Napoli. In Turkey, there are statues of

Statue of Athena. 2nd- 3rd century AD. Burdur Museum.

A view of the Temple of Athena at Assos, which was erected in 530 BC.

her in the İstanbul Archaeology Museums and Antalya Museum. Her symbols are spear, shield and aegis.

Her shield bore the head of the gorgon who transformed every onlooker to stone and was killed by Perseus. Her favorite animal was owl and favorite plant was olive. Goddess Athena was also treated in other branches of art. On vase illustrations, Athena's birth from the head of Zeus and Hephaestus's cleaving Zeus's head with an axe are featured.

Athena was recognized as Minerva in Rome. She was also called by the name Nike. Nike, the goddess who personified victory, was known to be the play mate of Athena. Even though Nike belongs with pre-Olympian deities, she was mostly associated with Athena. For example, the temple of Nike in Athens was assumed to be of Athena.

One of the most well-known libraries of the ancient times after the Library of Alexandria was the one in Pergamum. This library, which is situated near the temple of Athena, has a massive sculpture of the goddess Athena. This library was devoted to Athena. She was also revered as the chief deity in Troy, and a top-hill temple was built there for her. Unfortunately, this temple was destroyed during the excavations uncaringly carried out by Schliemann.

The Temple of Athens built at the acropolis of Assos in 530 BC, retains its ancient beauty. Many parts of this temple are at the İstanbul Archaeology Museums today. In Priene, there is an Ionic-order temple of Athena which was built by Pytheos the architect in the 4th century BC, with 6 x 11 columns and measuring 19.55 x 37.20 m. The eastern part of this temple was commissioned by Alexander the Great.

Temple of Athena, Priene. 4th century BC.

Furthermore, from the Temple of Athena in Pergamum, only the location of which can be discerned now, the propylon was dismantled and brought to Berlin and was re-assembled there at the Berlin Museum. The Temple of Athena at Heracleia, with its striking display reflected on the blue waters of Lake Bafa, has its walls still standing today. There are also other temples of Athena in Anatolia such as those in Side, Smyrna, Miletus, Phocaea and Erythrae.

The cult of Athena was experienced in Athens in its most intriguing form. The Panathenaic festival held to honor the goddess was an important event in a cultural, religious and artistic sense. Hence, the most important temples of her are to be found in Athens. The largest temple of Athena is the Temple of Parthenon constructed on the northern flank of the acropolis of Athens. This temple, which remains standing today in all its splendor, was created by architects Iktinos and

Kallikrates. It began to be built in 447 BC, and was completed in nine years. Its decorations, which can still be partially seen today, took six years. It has seventeen columns on the sides and eight of them on the front and back. On the south eastern corner of the Acropolis hill, across from this grandiose temple is the Temple of Athena Nike which survives to this day intact. The temple has embossments on it describing Greco-Persian wars and was built around 427-424 BC.

The most beautiful and largest of the temples in the Peloponnese is the Temple of Athena Alea in Tegea from the 4th century BC. Representing a blend of Doric, Ionic and Corinthian orders, the temple remains standing today, though damaged. Its architect was reportedly Scopas. The Temple of Athena Aphaea on the island of Aegina near Athens, which dates to the 5th century BC, is spectacular looking. This temple represents an association with the local god Aphaea. The third temple near the temples of Hera in Paestum in Italy is assumed to have been devoted to Athena.

Artemis of Versailles. Roman-era copy of a Hellenistic work.

ARTEMIS ⊢ DIANA

Artemis was the daughter of Zeus and Leto, and twin sister of Apollo. It was believed that Leto, after conceiving from Zeus, gave birth to her twins on the island of Delos.

Artemis was the goddess of pristine nature. She was the aide of women during childbirth, and the patron of animals. She strolled through the wilderness with arrows over her shoulder.

Artemis was called by many different epithets. Like her brother Apollo who represented the sun, Artemis represented the moon. She was called "Agrotera" the huntress goddess. She was also known as "Potnia Theron", the goddess of wild animals. As beautiful and good natured as she was, her anger was rampant. For instance, because King Admetos forgot to present offerings to her, she filled his nuptial chamber with snakes. She was angered by Meleager's father Oeneus and sent a boar to his land and made it eat the whole field. No mortal was able to touch Artemis, nor were they able to see her naked. Those who saw her naked, like Actaeon, suffered their punishment. Actaeon, who was raised by a centaur and was a good hunter like Artemis, claimed that he was actually better at hunting than she was. One day, Artemis and her nymphs went to a forest to cool off in the lake. Convinced that nobody would see them in this hidden corner, they all took their clothes off, immersed into the lake and began dancing. Before long, Actaeon heard their voices and went near them with his bow and arrow. Shrieking, the nymphs surrounded Artemis to hide the goddess from his eyes. At this moment, Artemis came out of the lake and approached this young man. She feared that he would tell everyone that he saw her and her nymphs naked. Therefore, she splashed some lake water on the face of this young man. At that moment, horns began to grow on the head of Actaeon, and he transformed into a stag. The hounds that were there devoured Actaeon right on the spot, in an excitement to find a prey. This is how Artemis brutally punished Actaeon for seeing her naked and claiming that he was a better hunter than her.

As maidens, girls would pray to Artemis, and in return, she would help them after marriage, during their childbirth. Artemis was at the same time the goddess of womanhood. She also symbolized the earth and fertility.

Homer refers to Ortygia as the birthplace of Artemis. Since Ortygia means quail in Greek, this place could be today's Bülbül Dağı (the Mount of the Nightingale). The people of Ephesus recorded that Ortygia was the name given to the woods near Ephesus, during the time of Tiberius. So, this goddess with complete Anatolian characteristics must have been related to Ephesus too.

The three-storey temple on the head of Artemis of Ephesus indicates that she is the guardian of cities as well as the wilderness. The crescent on her forehead symbolizes her virginity and that she is the goddess of the moon. Her multiple breasts are in reference to her being a goddess of fertility.

She was worshipped by the Romans mainly as Diana the goddess of moon and light. During the festival of Artemis held in the town of Caryae lying in the vicinity of Sparta, maidens danced wearing basket-like wreaths made from reeds. Sculpted females that function as columns in architecture were named after this theme as Caryatid. Diana of Versailles, showing her with a quiver over her shoulder and a stag near her, is the most famous statue of her. A Roman copy of this 4th-century-BC work is found at the Louvre Museum today. Also in this museum is a Roman copy of the Artemis of Gabii which is known to have been created by Praxiteles. Artemis of Ariccia, found at the Therme Museum in Rome is a copy of a sculpture dating to the 5th century BC. Artemis is mostly described in her sculptures with a quiver on her shoulder, and her hound and stag near her. In some of these depictions, Artemis holds a shining crescent in her hand, and in some of them she is seen with a wreath of stars around her head. Sometimes, this young and beautiful goddess is illustrated in her statues wearing a short garment revealing her bodily parts, and sometimes, holding a torch that symbolizes the moon. Animals that were offered to her were stags, hounds, roosters, partridges, bears, pigs and wolves. Laurel, myrtle, cypress and olive trees were the favorites of the beautiful goddess. To honor their goddess, the people of Ephesus built the Temple of Artemis which was one of the Seven Wonders of the World. This building was built over the holy site of Cybele, the mother goddess of Anatolia, and it measured 190 m. in length and 55 m. in width. It was the first marble structure made in the Ionic order. The temple with 127 columns had 36 of its columns decorated with embossments. One of these was created by the famed sculptor Scopas.

Artemis of Ephesus. 2nd century AD. Ephesus Museum.

Temple of Artemis at Sardis (Sardes). The temple was initiated in 300 BC, and went through three stages.

The altar in front of the temple was the work of Praxiteles. The sculptures of the monument of Amazons, which was inside, were created by the famous artists of Antiquity such as Polycleitus, Phidias, Kresilas and Kydon. The paintings at the temple were creations of Apelles of Ephesus. The first altar in this location, belonging to Artemis, was built in 652 BC; however, it was demolished during the attack of the Cimmerians. The Temple of Artemis–one of the seven wonders in the world–was built on this site around 564-546 BC. King Croesus of Lydia also assisted in the construction of it. The embossed column base which is at the British Museum today was a gift from him. Unfortunately, a crazy person named Herostratus set fire to this temple in 356 BC, on the night when Alexander the Great was born. During his campaign to Asia, Alexander the Great discovered that this temple was burnt on the night when he was born and wanted to contribute to its reconstruction, but the people of Ephesus returned his offer and rebuilt the Temple of Artemis themselves. Unfortunately, this building was pillaged during Christianity

and its stones were used in the construction of Hagia Sophia and Church of St. Jean in Ephesus. There are many other temples honoring Artemis in Anatolia. The Temple of Artemis that is located in Sardis the capital of Lydia was built in three different stages. The first temple was built around 300 BC, the second stage was from 175-150 BC, and the third stage corresponds to AD 150. Two columns remain standing from this temple today. The temples of Artemis in Side and Letoon are near those of her brother Apollo. The temples in Letoon describe Artemis with her quiver and arrows, and Apollo with his lyre. Artemis was worshipped in Perge as "Pergaia" meaning the Artemis of Perge. A temple of Artemis exists in Magnesia near Söke of the Aegean Region, built by Hermogenes–one of the greatest architects of his time–during the third quarter of the 2nd century BC. This temple measuring 41 x 67 m. was one of the foremost buildings of its time and had 8 x 15 columns and was ascended by 9 stairs. The frieze on the four sides of the temple, measuring 175 cm. in height, illustrates the war between the Greeks and Amazons in the form of an embossment. The embossments of this temple, which is in ruins today, are at the İstanbul Archaeology Museums. Artemis was later associated with Hecate and Selene.

APOLLO

Apollo, the god of the sun and light, was the son of Zeus and Leto. Leto's conception from Zeus caused Hera to harbor a great enmity towards her. Therefore, Leto always stayed away from Hera and her iniquities to be able to give birth to her baby healthily. The legend has it that, with the help of Zeus, Leto delivered her twins Artemis and Apollo, in Delos located at the center of the Cyclades islands. However, it is widely accepted that Apollo was born in the city of Patara in Lycia.

Homer's Iliad refers to Apollo as Lycian, which alludes to his Anatolian roots. Lycia, the land of sun and light, is located on today's Mediterranean coasts. The god of sun most likely came from Anatolia which is considered to be the land of the sun. Apollo is also found in the Hittite culture. Later, the cult of Apollo passed down from Anatolia to Greece and became popular there. Therefore, the people there associated it with their land and designated his birthplace as the islands. Apollo, like other things, came to Greece later. This is why, in the epic of Iliad, Apollo is portrayed as always taking the side of the Trojans and helping them. The cult of Apollo prevailed in many places of Anatolia, and received acceptance that was unparalleled by worship of other gods. It is seen that the cult of Apollo was also practiced ardently in the region of Troas over a long period of time. As told at the beginning of Iliad, Chryses, who was Apollo's priest, had her daughter captivated by Agamemnon. He attempted to salvage her daughter by offering gifts, only to be expelled and insulted by Agamemnon. So the priest pleaded with his god Apollo, "O god of the silver bow, that protects Chryse and holy Cilla and rulest Tenedos with thy might, hear me oh thou of Sminthe. If I have ever decked your temple with garlands, or burned your thigh-bones in fat of bulls or goats, grant my prayer, and let your arrows avenge these - my tears upon the Danaans." Apollo heard his cries and shot his arrows for nine consecutive days. This shows that around 1200 BC, when this war took place, the cult of Apollo existed and was ardently practiced in Anatolia. Apollo was worshipped here as the guardian of fields and named "Apollo Smintheus". The statues of the god Apollo usually have a mouse underneath the foot. He is called by many different names. Phoebos, meaning the shining one, is the

Apollo Belvedere. Roman-era copy of the original statue carved in the 4th century BC.

foremost among them. Xanthos meaning blonde, Chrysocome meaning the golden haired god, and Toxophoros meaning bow-bearer are all different names attributed to him. The god Apollo was referred to as the god of the silver bow many times. Lycegenes, which means noble in Lycia, was another name given to him referring to his Lycian origins. Apollo, who was also the god of foretelling and music, engaged in love affairs as well. One fine day, Apollo saw Daphne, the daughter of Peneus the river god, in Thessaly and lost his heart to her. But beautiful Daphne was sworn to remain a virgin. Therefore, she did not reciprocate his love. As the god Apollo ran towards her, she ran away fearing that she might violate her oath by falling in love with this handsome young man who was a total stranger to her. The beautiful girl pleaded with the Mother Earth to protect her as she was pursued by the god Apollo, and Mother Earth turned her into a bay (laurel) tree. Thus the bay tree became the sacred tree of this god from that day on. This love was immortalized by Bernini in the statue illustrating Apollo and Daphne.

Apollo lay with the daughter of a king, who was named Coronis, and this union produced Asclepius the god of medicine. However, this love ended in agony. The god of light and inspiration had many other love affairs like these. For instance, Apollo once fell in love with Cassandra, daughter of King Priam of Troy, granted her the gift of foretelling and prophecy at the Temple of Apollo in Thymbra near Troy. The priest of this temple was Laocoon. But Cassandra never returned Apollo's love. Therefore, he became outraged and swore that no one would believe her even though she could see the future. This curse was a very heavy burden on Cassandra. She foresaw the future but was unable to convince anybody. She even told that the wooden horse gifted to the Trojans was a scam and should not be accepted into the city, but nobody believed her. The horrible scenes from the future made her hair stand on end and drove her into the streets.

Apollo's union with Calliope, the highest of all muses, brought forth Orpheus who was a famous musician. Reportedly, a female soothsayer named Manto, who was from Colophon in Değirmendere near İzmir, bore him a son named Mopsus, also a seer. Mopsus became the foreteller of the prophecy center of Apollo in Clarus. He is also said to have fathered a child named Miletus from an Anatolian woman named Acacallis. This child reportedly established Miletus later on.

Marble statue of Apollo. 2nd century AD. Roman Period.

Apollo engaged in affairs with many other women and played many roles in legends. In one of these legends, he enters into a music competition against Marsyas the Silenos from Phrygia. A beautiful statue of Marsyas representing this theme is located at the İstanbul Archaeology Museums and another one is at Louvre.

Of the many temples built in Anatolia for Apollo, one is located in the antique city of Side within the provincial borders of Antalya. This temple, which was built during the second half of the 2nd century AD, was in the Corinthian order, had 6 x 11 columns and measured 16.37 x 29.50 m. There are also temples of Apollo in the antique cities such as Alabanda, Aegae and Hierapolis (Pamukkale). Apollo, as the god of light, gave light to both animate and inanimate beings. He was not only the source of life, but was also considered the god of fine arts. He would sometimes play the lyre and be seen dancing with the muses. Poets drew their inspiration from him. In his statues, Apollo is shown in a standing position, without a beard, young, sportsman-looking, healthy and generally nude. His curls fall down to his shoulders and he is seen with a lyre, arch and arrow. In his statues depicting him as a musician, he wears a loose, long and dangling chiton. His sacred animals were the swan, dolphin, crow and wolf, and his sacred plants were the bay tree, palm tree and olive tree.

The most well-known statue of the god Apollo is "Belvedere Apollo" which illustrates the moment after he slew the Python. This statue dating approximately to 350 BC, depicts Apollo's distinctive beauty. It is in the Vatican Museum today. "Apollo of Tenea", which dates to the 4th century BC, is in the Glyptohek Museum of Munich, "Apollo of Piombino", which dates to around 500 BC, is in the Louvre Museum, "Apollo Actius", which dates to the 6th century BC, is in the Louvre Museum, and "Apollo Sauroktonos (Apollo the Lizard Killer), which dates to around 350 BC and was carved by Praxiteles, is in the Vatican Museum of Rome. "Tiber Apollo" dating back to around 450 BC, which is in the National Museum of Rome, "Kassel Apollo" which is attributed to Phidias and is in the National Museum of Athens today, and the head statue of Apollo that once decorated the pediment of the Temple of Zeus in Olympia and is now in the Olympia Museum are some important works depicting Apollo.

Turkish museums, such as the ones in Ankara and Antalya, also have statues depicting Apollo. Especially important among them are the bronze sculpture at the Bursa Museum, and the sculpture of Apollo while playing

Head of the bronze Apollo statue. Roman-era copy of the 5ᵗʰ century-BC work. Bursa Museum.

Overleaf: Temple of Apollo at Didyma (300 BC-AD 200)

the lyre, which was found in Mileuts but is now exhibited at the İstanbul Archaeology Museums. The most famous prophecy center of Apollo in Greece is located in Delphi which is slightly inland from the northern coast of the Bay of Corinth. Apollo killed a dragon named Python in Delphi and established a prophecy center here. This temple dates back 373 BC, and was built in the place of an older temple. Some columns of this temple are standing today. Another temple of Apollo is in Bassae lying near Figaleia. Built on an isolated rocky hill wedged between the mountains of Arcadia, the temple dates back to the 4ᵗʰ century BC. Some decorations of the temple are exhibited at the British Museum. The oldest temple of Apollo

Temple of Apollo at Clarus. 3rd century BC.

is on a hilltop in Corinth which is a location established on the narrowest part of Continental Greece connecting it to the peninsula to its south. The monumental Doric temple of god Apollo dates back to 540 BC, with seven of its columns still visible today.

Clarus, mentioned previously, is one of the prophecy centers in Anatolia, which has been uncovered near Ahmetbeyli of İzmir with recent excavations. Measuring 26 x 46 m., the Doric-order temple was built in the beginning of the Hellenistic period and had six columns on its short side, and eleven columns on its long side. Colossal statues of Apollo, Artemis and Leto have been found at this temple. It was founded by a seer woman named Manto. The Temple of Apollo at Didyma is the most magnificent one dedicated to Apollo. Archaic Didymaion, the foundations of which were first laid in the end of the 8th century BC, was transformed into a large temple in the 6th century BC. King Croesus of

Lydia presented golden gifts to this temple. During the Ionian revolt, the Persians damaged this temple and even took the statue of Apollo, which was inside the temple, to Ekbatan. Once the Ionian cities were liberated after the triumph of Alexander the Great over the Persians, they began to be reconstructed. Temple of Apollo at Didyma was also reconstructed during this time. Around 300 BC, King Seleucus I of Syria brought back the statue that was taken to Ekbatan and presented it as a gift to the newly built temple. Built by Paeonius of Ephesus and Daphnis, the temple turned into a thrilling structure measuring 109.34 x 51.13 m. From the original 124 columns of the temple, those that still remain standing today can only hint at its past splendor.

Another prophecy center of Apollo is in Patara, his birthplace. This served as the center of prophecy during winter; and in summer, the one in Delos was used. Located in Letoon near Patara are the temples of Leto, Apollo and Artemis lying side by side.

ARES ᴴ MARS

In Hesiod's Theogony, Ares, who was the son of Zeus and Hera, symbolized brute force and terrifying warfare. As a god who delighted in bloodshed or desired to sack fortresses, he was not revered much. He had epithets such as the one that destroys (Anaieres) and the one that causes tears (Polydakrys). He was accompanied by murderous creatures on the battle field. His sister Eris the goddess of strife and his two sons he begat from Aphrodite, who were named Deimos (dread) and Phobos (fear), would be near him. The Keres who were the death spirits and Kydoimos (Cydoemus) who was the symbol of confusion were also his company.

Homer describes him as a troublemaker to humankind who demolishes castles and has blood on his hands. In the Iliad, Zeus speaks of this sinister son of his as follows:

"Most hateful to me art you of all gods that hold Olympus,
For ever is strife dear to you and wars and fighting. You have the
unbearable, unyielding spirit of your mother Hera, Her can I scarce
control by my words."

Ares was not smart like Athena. He would raise strife imprudently and would like to perpetuate it. Athena was smart, cunning, and those that she sided with would triumph because she knew that trickery was at least as important as courage in fighting. During the Trojan War, when gods were divided into two and joined fighting, Ares was wounded by a Greek named Diomedes whom Athena was helping. As is known, after Troy fell due to the scam of the wooden horse, a ferocious massacre ensued. In one instance, Athena wounded him with a stone, and he was helpless before Athena, despite being the god of warfare.

Being so disliked among the mortals, Ares ironically won the heart of Aphrodite the goddess of love. However, he fell flat on his face in this matter as well. He made his watchman Alectryon guard the door so as not to be caught while he was inside with Aphrodite; however, his guard fell asleep and failed to warn them of the danger. As a result, Helios the god of sun saw what they were doing and informed Aphrodite's

Bronze statue of Mars found at the house of Poseidon in Zeugma, in 2000.

husband Hephaestus. The ironmonger god tied them tightly to the bed and ensured that the rest of the gods saw this disgrace. Thus, this callow rascal made a fool out of himself. And the watchman Alectryon paid the penalty by being transformed into a rooster after that day. This is why a rooster crows every morning after seeing the sun. When, on a hillside, Poseidon's son Halirrhothius assaulted Ares's daughter Alcippe, whom Ares begat from Aglaulushe, he was killed by Ares. In response to this, Poseidon gathered the Olypian gods near this hill to try Ares, and the gods acquitted him. After this trial, the hill was named Areopagus meaning the Hill of Ares.

Ares begat a son named Cycnus from Pelopea the daughter of Pelias, who was a ruthless bandit. Robbing whomever he came across, this bandit was finally killed by Heracles. He also wounded Ares who came to the aid of his son. According to legend, the Amazons were the daughters of Ares.

There is a temple of Ares in Thebes, and ancient records also mention a temple dedicated to him around the agora in Athens. The oldest depictions of him are on Archaic vases having black paintings. These paintings render him as armed from head to toe and having a beard. In his later sculptures, he is seen as a more idealized young man in the nude. He wears a headpiece in these sculptures, the only thing alluding to his epithet of warrior. Since Ares did not have distinctive characteristics, sculptors strived to create new forms in representing him. The form of depiction known as "Ares Borghese" has been admired for centuries and the sculpture which gave its name to this new form is in the Louvre Museum.

The most well-known sculpture of Ares is known as "Ludovisi Ares". This sculpture, which is in the Therme Museum of Rome today, depicts him as seated. He is nude and only a piece of cloth covers his waist. The sculpture, on which Lysippus's influences can be traced, illustrates Ares with both of his hands placed on one knee, together with his shield near him and Eros between his feet.

Unlike in Greece, Ares was much revered in Rome. He was known as Mars in Latin, and the council of priests at his temple in Rome guarded the two shields of Mars and held feasts every year to honor this god of war. The greatest temple of Mars in Rome is "Mars Vindicator" built by Emperor Augustus. Animals such as bulls, boars and rams were presented to him as offerings. His sacred animals were the rooster and vulture.

A vase image showing Ares while fighting. 5th century BC.

Depiction of Hephaestus and a satyr on a vase. 435-430 BC.

HEPHAESTUS ¼ VULCANUS

Hephaestus, the god of fire and manufacturing, was the son of Zeus and Hera according to Homer. Hesiod merely records that he was born of Hera. Reportedly, Hera was outraged that Zeus gave birth to Athena from his head and in return, gave birth to Hephaestus alone with the help of plant extracts.

While Zeus punished Hera by chaining and hanging her upside down, for what she had done to Heracles, he expelled Hephaestus from Olympus because he sided with his mother in the dispute over the Trojan War. Hephaestus became lame when Zeus tossed him from Olympus holding his leg. Hera was also ashamed of having such an ugly child, so she flung him from Olympus into the sea. He was rescued and raised by Eurynome, the daughter of Oceanus and Tethys. Living in a cave for 9 years, Hephaestus mused over his revenge to his mother, made plans, and created unprecedented tools. One day, he sent his mother a magical golden throne, which he especially designed for her. The throne was so spectacular that Hera immediately sat on it and was immediately entrapped by it. Hera was not able to be rescued by the deities or even by herself. In an attempt to save his mother, Ares tried to bring Hephaestus to Olympus; however, the ironmonger god drove him off by his flames. Hephaestus accepted to release his mother Hera on two conditions. The first was to be reaccepted to Olympus, and the second was to marry Aphrodite.

After his two conditions were met, Hephaestus's resentments passed, so he returned to Olympus together with Dionysus the god of wine and released Hera.

Even though all the deities were beautiful, Hephaestus was an exception. He overcame this weakness of his by building a gleaming bronze palace for himself and marrying Aphrodite –the most beautiful goddess. He also devoted himself to art and built palaces and crafted thrones and wands. Thus he led his life in Olympus.

After the creation of man, Zeus assigned the task of creating a woman to Hephaestus. He made the bedroom of Zeus and Hera, Zeus's shield

Goddess Thetis and Hephaestus.
490 BC.

and wand, Poseidon's trident fishing spear, Heracles's golden armor, Achilles's shield and Helios's golden chariot.

Hephaestus learned from Helios the god of sun that his wife Aphrodite was cheating on him with Ares. He prepared a bed that would entrap them both in nets and departed as if heading for Lemnos. When he unexpectedly came home, Ares and Aphrodite were waiting for him entangled in nets. He took his revenge by humiliating them before all deities. His beautiful wife Aphrodite was not faithful to him, but he also pursued other women regardless of his ugliness. He actually tried hard to seduce Athena. Ugly as he was, he managed to marry Aglaea -the youngest of the Charites- besides Aphrodite the goddess of beauty.

The fire god of volcanoes, Hephaestus was also aided by certain secondary deities. Cyclops, for instance, constantly helped him by

Return of Hephaestus to Olympus, with Dionysus and his retinue.
Side A of an Attic red-figure pelike, 440–430 BC.

hammering. The fire god Hephaestus is depicted in his statues with a strong and large body, with muscled arms and a hairy chest. He has untidy hair and pointed beard, and he is depicted with a leather cap and a worker's garment leaving one of his shoulders open. He is sometimes seen while holding a hammer and pincer. Hephaestus was known as Vulcanus in Rome. Even though he is illustrated as lame in archaic sculptures, this characteristic was not depicted later. There is a spectacular temple of Hephaestus in Athens, to the north west of the acropolis. Dating to the 5th century BC, this temple still mesmerizes the onlookers today. There is also a temple of him in Paestum, Italy.

Old records state that the eternal flame burning on a mountain in Çıralı near Olympus, in the Lycia Region, was also a temple of his.

HERMES · MERCURIUS

Every night after his wife Hera went to sleep, Zeus the king of gods would secretly meet with Maia, the daughter of Pleione from the lineage of the Titans. Their meeting place was a cave on Mount Cyllene south of Arcadia. Hermes came into the world as the fruit of this union. This newborn had extraordinary characteristics. Even as a baby, he began to run away from home and get involved in mischief.

One day, while he was wandering away from his home, a tortoise caught his sight. With a knife, he cleaned out the shell and stretched seven strings made from sheep intestines across it. Thus he made a lyre and began to play this new instrument. After a while, he became hungry. Towards the evening, he arrived at the pastures in Pieria where Apollo's animals grazed, and stole fifty cows from there. Lest somebody would find out his theft and trace him, he made the cows walk backwards. He, too, wore the sandals woven from tree branches and erased his foot prints by walking backwards. Still, Apollo discovered that his cattle were stolen after a while. As soon as he learned who the thief was, he found Hermes in his crib. Apollo wrathfully walked towards the little child, who stole his cattle, and as he stepped on a stringed musical instrument made from a tortoise shell, he realized the pleasant sounds coming out of it. He forgave Hermes in return for this instrument. Later, he also awarded Hermes a golden wand for the lyre he invented. Thus, Hermes became the guardian of thieves. Sophocles's play Ichneutae, in which he talks about the first theft of Hermes, was first staged around 450 BC. Before long, Zeus accepted this crafty son of his into Olympus and made him his messenger. It was Hermes who brought the golden apple to Paris on Mount Ida, during the beauty contest between the goddesses. He is mostly characterized as a guide in legends. The messenger of gods begat many children. Hermes worked as a shepherd on the mountains of Arcadia in order to have the girl that he loved, and finally married her. From this marriage came forth Pan. This child was different with his goat's feet, horns and tail. He played the flute very well when he grew up, roamed the grasslands and became the god of the wild. Hermes was also the god of merchants. But before all else, Hermes was the god of shepherds and fertility of animals. The representation of this epithet of his is Kriophoros (Hermes carrying a ram). He also took the spirits of the

Statue of Hermes holding the child Dionysus.

Hermes tying his sandals. Roman-era copy of a 4th century BC-work. Antalya Museum.

dead to Hades. Due to this duty, he was also known as Psychopomps, meaning "the guide of the souls". Various depictions of Hermes were made representing his duties.

He usually wore the invisibility helmet of Hades, and winged sandals that allowed him to travel quickly, and held a wand entwined by two serpents (kerykaion) and a golden pouch. In his archaic depictions, he is seen as a bearded, mature person. In his classical-era depictions, he was shown as a young man with an agile and energetic body. In Praxiteles's sculpture of Hermes dating to the 4th century BC, he is holding Dionysus with his right arm. This sculpture, which is one of the best of Hermes, is in the Olympia Museum today. Another sculpture of Hermes, which is of matching beauty, was created by Lysippos and is in the Naples Museum

Head statue of Hermes found in 1959 in Side. Roman Period.

currently. A Roman copy of the sculpture of Hermes created by Alcamenes around 430 BC, is in the İstanbul Archaeology Museums. The bronze sculpture of his in the Naples National Archaeological Museum, which was created by Lysippos and is known as "Resting Hermes", is also very important. He holds a money pouch in his left hand, and there are wings at his ankles. He is sitting on a rock.

A sculpture of Hermes depicting him while orating (Hermes Logios) is at Villa Ludovisi in Rome. The plants devoted to him were myrtle tree, olive tree and opium poppy. He was known as Mercurius in Rome. The group in bronze of Mercury and Psyche, created by Adriaan de Vries, can be seen in the Louvre Museum in Paris. In paintings, scenes were chosen based on Ovid.

HESTIA ⋈ VESTA

The symbol of hearth, Hestia was the daughter of Cronus and Rhea, and sister of Zeus, Hera, Demeter, Poseidon and Hades. This goddess represented the hearth of a home and thus she had an altar in every household. She was also considered to be the guardian of posterity, cities and the state.

The fire at the Temple of Apollo at Delphi symbolized the religious union of Greece. Because Hestia was revered by both deities and humans, Olympian gods always offered her a seat before taking a seat themselves. But this respect did not spoil the goddess; she did not interfere with the business of the other gods. Since she never left Olympus, she never became the subject of legends.

Hestia was the embodiment of a symbol, rather than a person. When Poseidon wanted to marry her, she sought the protection of Zeus and professed that she intended to keep her virginity. She swore to stay as a virgin and lived up to her oath. She was known more as Vesta in Rome, where temples were erected in her name. The maidens accepted into the temples of Vesta were forced to keep their virginities all their life and those who violated this custom would be punished by being buried in soil alive.

Hestia was accepted as the regulator of family life, and provider of peace and happiness. Therefore, her holy fire burning at the Temple of Apollo at Delphi was taken to newly found homelands. Lacking in significant numbers, the temples of Hestia were all built to a circular plan.

She was depicted as serious, wearing long garments and with her head covered. Her signs were her wand, sacrifice bowl and flames. There are not many statues of Hestia. The statue of Hestia created by Glaucus of Argos for the city of Olympia is famous. The most well-known statue of her, on the other hand, was located in Paros.

Depiction of the goddess Hestia on a vase, dating to 520 BC.

DIONYSUS = BACCHUS

Known as Bacchus during the Roman period, the symbol of nature and god of wine Dionysus appears as a deity influencing art, social life and religion starting from the 6th century BC. Neither Homer nor Hesiod talks much about Dionysus, who was a latecomer among the immortals of Olympus.

Only a few centuries after these authors, in the 5th century BC, Euripides introduces him in his work named "The Bacchae". From this century onwards, the cult of god Dionysus developed and became widespread.

The warmhearted chief of the gods, Zeus, fell in love with Semele -the daughter of the Theban king Cadmus- and seduced her and made love to her after awhile. Semele became pregnant during this union in love.

Zeus's jealous wife Hera found out about this and wanted to take revenge. Hera disguised herself as the old nursing mother of Semele and went near her. She gave her some advice. She said that now that Semele was able to steal the heart of Zeus as a mortal girl, she could well plead with Zeus and make him appear fully as a god to her, with all his splendor. If he loved him, he would accept to appear to her as he does to his wife. Jealous Hera accomplished what she had in mind; it was now instilled in Semele's head to see Zeus as he actually is.

If this plan succeeded, Semele would be destroyed. Before long, Semele began to plead with Zeus. She asked him to appear as a god. Zeus had sworn her that he would do what she wanted. Therefore, he could not resist the requests of his lover and appeared to her as god. The appearance of Zeus caused poor Semele to burn. She miscarried her seven-month-old baby while she burnt.

Zeus hid this baby in his calf, secretly from his wife Hera. When the time was right, the baby, who was to be named Dionysus, came into

Sculpture of Dionysus and Satyr. This Roman-era work was found in the upper agora of Sagalassos. Burdur Museum.

Dionysus, together with a satyr and the Maenads.
2nd century-AD. Antakya Museum.

the world. He ordered the messenger god Hermes to take the child
to the nymphs of Nysa to be raised by them. On Nysa Hill, rivers of
cold water ran in dense forests. The nymphs accepted the child

whom Hermes brought to be given to their keeping, and raised him meticulously. As Dionysus grew up, the grapevine in front of the cave that was used as his house also grew, yielding large bunches of grapes. Dionysus grew into an exuberant young man pacing through the forest to hunt. One day, Dionysus collected grapes from the grapevine, squeezed them and made wine from their juice. He and the nymphs drank this wine and held lively and joyful carnivals. They wore wreaths made of grapevine leaves during these carnivals. The retinue of Dionysus was known as "Thiasus".

These carnivals were attended by the Bacchae, who were the female followers of Dionysus, the Nymphs, who were the daughters of Zeus, the Satyrs, who were woodland and mountain spirits, as well as Sileni, who were very wise and musically talented. Later, Dionysus scoured the globe to introduce wine to people as a source of consolation if drunk modestly. On Naxos Island, he found Ariadne whom Theseus left behind. He married her and begat children from her. He came through the islands to Egypt, and from there to Phrygia of Anatolia. He also made love to Althaea, the wife of king of Calydon, and from this union came forth Deianeira who later became the wife of Heracles.

The cult of Dionysus seems to have become widespread in Greece in the 5th century BC. In Euripides's Bacchae, Dionysus is quoted as saying "Far now behind me lies the golden ground of Lydian and of Phrygian". He is presented as the god of Lydia and Phrygia. Even though it was later accepted in mythology that Dionysus was born of Semele, he was actually an Anatolian deity. The cult of Dionysus, which was initially widespread in Anatolia, must have gone to Greece from there. In the region of Lydia, which corresponds to the Manisa-Salihli area, viniculture is practiced today. In fact, viniculture is practiced in all parts of western Anatolia, where in autumn, vine harvest carnivals are still held as in old days. Dionysus was a god of nature.

Among plants, he symbolized those that affect humans and guide their life the most. He lived on the mountains together with wild animals. Being a god and human being, the wine god established the relationship between humans and nature.

The mosaic of Drunken Dionysus at the Antakya Museum clearly reflects his human side.

Dionysus Temples

Formerly, Dionysus was depicted as wearing a long garment, a wreath of ivies on his head, holding a wine cup and a wand, and bearded and long haired. However, after the 4th century BC, he began to be depicted as a young man with his beautiful and delicate curly hair falling on his shoulders. Animals devoted to him were bulls, donkeys, goats, peacocks, deer, tigers and magpies.

The most important temple of him is in Teos near Seferihisar, İzmir. The largest Dionysus Temple of the antiquity is in ruins today. This temple has six columns on its short side and twelve columns on its long side, measures 18.50 x 35.00 m. and is in the Ionic order. It was constructed in the 2nd century BC, by the famous architect Hermogenes. The temple that is seen today is the section surviving after the modifications and repairs during the periods of Augustus and Hadrianus. The theater, just as the temple and other places, was constructed against a natural setting.

There is an altar dedicated to Dionysus in the theaters, and many theater scenes are decorated with embossments of Dionysus. Furthermore, the Ionian Actors Union was also founded in Teos towards the end of the 3rd century BC; the actors used Teos as their center but also performed shows in other places. These were important elements of Dionysus carnivals. Another temple worth mentioning is the temple of Dionysus with its poetic beauty near the theatre in Pergamum. The People of Pergamum erected this temple on the terrace of the theatre, overlooking the neighborhood.

It was built in the 2nd century BC, representing the best example of Hellenistic-era temples. Rising on top of a podium, the Ionic order temple measures 11.80 x 20.22 m. The temple was accessed by 25 steps which reach 4.5 m. in height. The four exquisite columns in the front reflected the beauty of the temple. The temple of Dionysus in Pergamum went through great change during the Roman period.

Repairs were made during the period of Caracalla (AD 211-217), and former andesite coating of the temple was replaced with marble. After the aids given to their city by Caracalla, the people of Pergamum began worshipping him as the "New Dionysus". There are small Dionysus temples in the agora of antique Assos and antique city of Side.

Overleaf:
Mosaic of the drunken Dionysus.
Dionysus shown while taking a step forward with seemingly shaky legs.
Antakya Museum.

DEITIES AROUND ZEUS

There were many deities surrounding Zeus including Themis, the Charites, the Muses, Eros, Nike, Iris, Hebe, Eileithyia and Eris. Let us introduce them briefly here:

Themis

Themis, a female Titan, was the daughter of Uranus and Gaia. She became the second wife of Zeus after Metis.

Next he married bright Themis,
who bore the Horae:
Eunomia, Dike and blooming Eirene,
who minds the works of mortal men,
and the Moirae, to whom wise Zeus gave the greatest honor,
Clotho and Lachesis and Atropos,
who give mortal men evil and good to have.

This is how Hesiod tells of the marriage of Themis to Zeus and their children. Themis lived in Olympus with Zeus, advised him and assisted him. She organized ceremonies, called deities to meetings, ensured the ethical order among human beings, and counseled other deities. She was accepted as the goddess of justice. She was the legislation, the rule and the law itself, the godly law that was not transitory. She lived in Olympus and chaired the meetings of the gods. She was at the same time the mother of the Horae, whom she had by Zeus. The Horae were the three goddesses of climate and time. Their duty was to open and close the gates of Olympus and serve Hera. According to Hesiod, of the three Horae, Eunomia symbolized the good order, Dike symbolized fairness and justice, and Eirene symbolized peace. In the Hellenistic period, these three Horae became four and represented the four seasons. The Horae were illustrated holding a flower or a fruit in their hands. Themis was shown in her statues as a serious and demure woman. She had an esteemed place among the deities but there is no legend that is specifically about her. She is the goddess of eternal and infinite law and thus her symbol is a pair of scales.

Muses

The nine muses, who were spirits presiding over inspiration and art, were born from the union of Zeus and Uranus's daughter Mnemosyne the

Statue of the muse Melpomene. Aphrodisias Museum.

goddess of memory. These spirits were known as the Mousa in Greek and Musa in Latin. These nine muses were born after nine nights of love and they lived in Olympus. Led by the Charites and Himeros, they sang songs and praised the gods. Homer deemed the muses as the goddesses of music who created joy at the tables of the gods. Muses have different powers and signs.

Calliope, who was considered to be the head of them, was the guardian of epic poetry and legends. Her sign was a beautiful writing tablet and a pointed pen. She was known as the muse of eloquence. Clio was the guardian of history writers and her sign was a flute. Thaelia was the muse of comedy and was symbolized by the comedy mask. Melpomene was the muse of tragedy and was considered to be the guardian of tragedy from the end of the Hellenistic Period. She was depicted with a tragedy mask. Terpsichore represented dancing. Her symbol was a lyre. Erato was the muse of lyric poetry. Urania was the muse of astronomy and her symbol was a globe. Polhymnia was in charge of religious poetry and her sign was pantomime.

All of the bards and musicians on the earth drew inspiration from Apollo and the Muses. The words museum and music also derives from Greek mousa. The muses do not have a legend specific to them. They played the role of singers in all the celebrations of the gods. The oldest song of the muses was the one they sang to celebrate the birth of a new order after the triumph of the Olympian gods over the Titans.

Charites

Charites were goddesses inspiring artistic activities and symbolizing what appeals to the eye. Their name derives from the word Charis meaning shine, glitter and beauty. They were the three daughters of Zeus from Oceanus's daughter Eurynome. This is how Hesiod tells of this marriage:

And Eurynome, the daughter of Ocean,
beautiful in form,
bare him three fair-cheeked Charites (Graces),
Aglaea, and Euphrosyne, and lovely Thaleia

They were the personifications of all things that beautify not only nature but also human life. They symbolized everything that seems beautiful to the eye. They were therefore representations of the nature which gives flowers and fruits. For this reason, they are often confused with the

Embossment of Mousa playing the lyre. 2nd century BC.
Istanbul Archaeology Museums.

Horae. They were included in the retinues of Apollo, Aphrodite and Dionysus. They rejoiced human beings and gods. Their names and numbers varied depending on the region and periods. Aglaea, the youngest of the Charites, symbolized shine. Euphrosyne represented joy and happiness. Thaleia represented blooming. These young and lovely girls, who were the guardians of all sorts of art, were first described as wearing long garments and flower wreaths. They too lived in Olympus together with the Muses. They sometimes formed choruses with them. The Charites, who were in the retinue of god Apollo, were generally illustrated as three naked young girls, resting their arms on one another. This depiction of them was created especially after the 4th century BC. Charites were goddesses who inspired and protected alls sorts of art works and who aroused creativity in humans and gods.

Nike

Nike was a goddess who symbolized victory. She was born from the Titan Pallas and Oceanus's daughter Styx. She was illustrated as a fast-flying winged girl. Even though Nike belonged to the generation of gods prior to the Olympian gods, latter writers assumed her to be the play mate of Athena. Some accept Nike as an additional name of Athena too. Because Nike helped Zeus in his war against the Titans, she was accepted as a symbol of victory besides Athena. The Temple of Athena-Nike in Athens was devoted to her, so that victory never left their city. Nike, in Athens, was no more than another epithet of Athena.

Iris

Iris was one of the goddesses who represented light. She was the daughter of Thaumas and Electra, and sister of the Harpies. She was an Oceanid paternally and maternally. Iris symbolized the rainbow and at the same time served as a messenger like Hermes. She was at the service of Zeus and Hera mostly. She had wings, and was depicted as covered with a fine tulle reflecting the colors of the rainbow under the sun. She was sometimes shown as the wife of Zephyrus and mother of Eros. Homer speaks of Iris in the Iliad as "fleet as the wind". Iris was depicted as a beautiful and young girl with wings.

Hebe

Hebe, who symbolized youth, was the daughter of Zeus and Hera. Her main duty was serving drinks to gods. Later, the task of serving drinks to gods was given to Ganymede of Troy whom Zeus abducted. Hebe was characterized more as a girl skilled at house chores. In the Iliad, she is depicted while preparing her mother Hera's chariot and washing her brother Ares who came from war. She was also depicted while dancing to the lyre of Apollo, together with the Muses and Horae. Hebe married Heracles who rose to Olympus after his death. She symbolized eternal youth

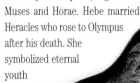

near Heracles, who was the symbol of heroism, courage and power.

Eileithyia

She was the daughter of Zeus and Hera, and sister of Hephaestus and Hebe. Eileithyia was the midwife goddess who took care of childbirth. She gave the pregnant women their labor pains and help with delivery. When she was late, the birth would be difficult. As she never went against what her mother Hera said, she did not attend the labor of Leto and Alcmene while they delivered their children because these babies were from their extramarital affairs with Zeus. In her depictions, she is covered with a tulle from head to toe. She extends one hand to help, and holds a torch in her other hand. Sometimes she was shown as kneeling down.

Nike of Samothrace.
The sculpture dating to 220 BC is in the Louvre Museum.

Embossment of Hecate from the Altar of Zeus in Pergamum.

Eros

Eros, or Cupido as in Latin, originated as a natural power that ensured union and reproduction in the universe created by Gaia after Chaos. However, later, Eros came to be accepted as the son of Aphrodite and Hermes. He was shown as the son of either Iris or Eileithyia in other legends. Eros found a way of reaching his goal; however, he was not an almighty god, rather a power in constant anxiety due to dissatisfaction. He was shown as a little child with wings. He shot arrows of love into the

hearts and made people fall in love. He was known as Amor in Rome. The
story of Eros and Psyche as told in Apuleius's Metamorphosis has been a
folkloric theme throughout the world. In this story, which is based on a
legend set in Miletus, Eros represents love and passion, while Psyche
represents the soul. Soul and love are two inseparable elements. Eros, a
lovely young boy, is depicted as having two wings on his back, and
holding an arrow and arch. Whomever he shot with his arrows would burn
with the fire of love. This is how Eros was illustrated in sculptures. He was
also a commonly used figure in sarcophagi.

Eris

Eris, the goddess of fighting and strife was born from Nyx (the night). In fact, the troublesome and destructive gods and goddesses were all born from the night. Eris was born after the gods of vengeance, deception, resentment and betrayal, all of whom terrorized humans. She was generally accepted as the sister and companion of Ares. Hesiod presents some abstract concepts such as hardship (Ponos), pain (Algos), hunger (Limos), forgetfulness (Lethe) and oath (Horkos) as her children.

This goddess is featured in the story of the beauty contest between the three goddesses. Eris was not invited to the wedding of Peleus and Thetis lest she would cause a conflict. This had upset her, and she decided to take her revenge; she wrote on an apple "to the most beautiful one" and presented it to the goddesses. As is known, Athena, Hera and Aphrodite all claimed the apple, each arguing that she was "the most beautiful one". When they were unable to make a decision, they asked Zeus for help. Zeus assigned Paris, the shepherd of Mount Ida, as referee and avoided this sensitive task. In the end, the first beauty contest of the world took place on Mount Ida. Consequently, the bribing during the contest, by offering the most beautiful woman of the world, caused the Trojan War. Eris was usually described as having wings and in the form of a female spirit, who resembled the Erinyes and Iris.

Hecate

Hecate was a mysterious goddess with no specific myth to her name. Homer does not refer to her, but Hesiod's Theogony cites her name. Hecate comes from the sun line of the Titans. Hecatebolos, one of the main titles defining Apollo and Artemis, means the "far-shooting". For Romans, she was very interesting and much revered, and was known as the goddess of moon and the queen of dark powers that ruled over the night and darkness. She is featured in the Aenid written by Virgil. She was born from the Titan Perses and Asterie, who was the daughter of Coeus and Phoebe. She was special for Zeus. At war, whomever Hecate wished to grant victory would become victorious. She would stand beside the kings on social occasions. Hecate was an Anatolian goddess and passed to Greece from Anatolia. She became associated with Artemis, Selene and Persephone.

Sea hunters would recite her name along with that of Poseidon. Hecate resembled Artemis of Ephesus very much because she appeared to be another version of Artemis. There is a temple of Hecate in the antique city of Lagina near Yatağan. Most of the friezes of this temple, which are themed on the Amazons, are in the İstanbul Archeology Museums today.

Terracotta figurine of flying Eros, found in Tralles. 2ⁿᵈ century BC.

Oceanus

Oceanus, who was born to Gaia, the Mother Earth, and Uranus, was the first one of the twelve titan children of Gaia. However, Oceanus did not take part in the war of the Titans and settled in a far end of the world. Oceanus was a universal river that circled all the lands and seas. He was the origin of lakes, rivers and spring waters. Later, he gave his name to large seas, such as the Atlantic Ocean. The sun rose from the waves of Oceanus and set on the waves of him. Oceanus lived with his sisters, and his wife Thetis, in a far end of the world. For this reason, he would not participate in the meetings of the gods in Olympus. He only accepted the superiority of Zeus among gods. He was shown as a kindhearted old man. In depictions of plastic arts, he appears grand despite his old age. He was depicted gorgeously in the mosaics of the Antakya Museum and Zeugma mosaics in Gaziantep. On his head, he has the horn of a bull which was the unchangeable sign of the river gods, and a foot of a crustacean which was the symbol of the sea gods. His marriage with Thetis produced more than three thousand female creatures. Hesiod tells that, these include Electra, Doris, Clymene, Dione, Perse, Metis, Eurynome, Calypso and Tyche. Among these creatures, Styx was the oldest. When every god was allocated their share, he was the first to arrive in Olympus. It symbolized the underground river.

Achelous

Achelous, who was the oldest son of Oceanus and Thetis, symbolized the largest river of Greece. The marriage of Achelous and Melpomene, a muse, brought forth the Sirens, who were half women and half birds. Achelous has been a subject of numerous legends. For example, in order to take Deianira, the daughter of the king of Calydon, he fought against Heracles. When he was beaten, he disguised firstly as a snake and then a bull; however, he could not escape from Heracles.

After Heracles beat him, he also tore his horn. In order to take his horn back, Achelous had to give Amalthea's cornucopia, which scattered flowers and fruits. In some of the depictions, his body was shown as a bull and his head was shown as that of a bearded human. In some of them, he was depicted in the exact opposite way.

Sculpture of the river god. 2nd century AD. Istanbul Archaeology Museums.

Oceanus Mosaic. 2nd century AD. Antakya Museum.

Nymphs

Nymphs, who were deemed goddesses of secondary importance, were still effective and powerful on humans and nature. For that reason, they were called by epithets such as glorious and great, like other goddesses. In fact "nymph" means bride but it was the name given to the females of the godlike and natural creatures living in moorlands, water and forests. Nymphs, who were the daughters of Zeus, participated in the meetings of the gods in Olympus. Although they were not immortal, they fed on ambrosia and thus had boundless beauty and youth. Nymphs were related to the gods such as Zeus, Hermes, Apollo and Dionysus. The real friends of the nymphs, who lived in nature, were Panes, Satyrs, Sirens and Priapus.

Nymphs were named according to their place and function in nature.

Spirits such as Dryads, Hamadryads, Naiads and Oreads were accepted as nymphs. The daughters of Nereus were also nymphs. Circe, who is mentioned in the Odyssey, was famous for witchcraft. She was born to Helios, the sun god, and Perse, the daughter of Oceanus. In some of the legends, she is said to be the daughter of Hecate and to have learned witchcraft from her. She is mentioned not only in the Odyssey but also in the myth of the Argonauts. Another nymph, who loved Odysseus, was Calypso. The name suggests 'hiding, covering' in Greek. She loved Odysseus very much and kept him on the island of Ogygia. The gods, who felt pity for Odysseus, told Calypso to send him to his country. She unwillingly did what gods wanted her to. Today in Malta, there is a beautiful bay named Calypso Bay.

Naiads

Naiads were water nymphs symbolizing rivers. Nymphaeum, which are large fountains in Ancient cities, must have derived from the word nymph.

Dryads

Dryads were nymphs of trees. The word "dryad" means oak. Eurydice, the wife of the famous musician Orpheus, was a Dryad. Hamadryads were also tree nymphs. Oreads were mountain nymphs. They frequently escaped from men. For that reason, they were among the huntresses of Artemis.

Nereus and the Daughters of Nereus

Nereus was born from the union of Pontus (sea) with his mother Gaia (earth). Nereus married Doris, the daughter of Oceanus, and they had fifty daughters in this marriage. In mythology, these girls are known as the Nereids. These girls are frequently mentioned in the epics by Homer and Hesiod. They symbolized the foamy waves, colors and different phases of the seas, and they became the subject of many legends. The Nereids lived with their father in a palace at the bottom of the sea; sometimes they played with waves and sometimes they swam with dolphins. The palace of Nereus was in a cave off the coast of Cnidus in the Aegean Sea. Nereus was known as the old man of the sea. Like other water deities, Nereus also had the ability of foresight. In art, he was depicted as an old man with seaweed hair and with a baton in his hand.

The most famous daughter of Nereus was Amphitrite, the wife of Poseidon. There are sculptures and architectural elements depicting the Nereids. For example, there used to be Nereid Sculptures between the columns of the Nereid Monument which was made around 400 BC in Xanthos. This monument, which was dismantled and taken to the British Museum and was restored there, has an extraordinary beauty. Because of the Nereid sculptures between the columns, the monument was called the Nereid Monument.

Sirens

Sirens were mermaids. They were believed to have a woman's body, bird wings and a beautiful voice. In Medieval times, they were accepted as half-human and half-fish creatures that had no wings. Sirens were the daughters of the river Achelous and the muse Melpomene. They used to sing beautiful songs and sailors could not resist their beautiful voices, which called them to the direction of the Sirens. This would result in the Sirens capturing them and cutting them into pieces.

While Odysseus was turning to his land from Troy, he passed through the lands of the Sirens. Following the advice of Circe, he blocked the ears of his shipmen with beeswax and saved himself and his crew. The Argonauts also survived the Sirens during their voyage. The melodies coming from the lyre of Orpheus, who was also on the Argo ship, dazzled the Sirens, and they threw away their instruments to the sea and listened to the lyre of Orpheus. It was also told that Demeter transformed them into birds because they failed to take care of her daughter, Persephone. Another rumor has it that the Sirens begged to the gods to have wings in order to search for their friend Persephone around the world. In time, they came to be thought as fish-tailed creatures with a woman's body.

Triton

Triton was the son of Poseidon and Amphitrite. He lived in a golden palace beneath the waves, together with his mother and father, arousing fear. Triton was depicted as half human, half fish and sometimes as a dolphin. He would ride on the waves in his chariot. Triton showed the Argonauts the way to the Black Sea; this is about his only role in the legends. In addition to his father's palace, he also lived in Lake Tritonis of Libya. He had a daughter named Pallas, who features in the legend of Athena. Sometimes, Triton was used as a common name for multiple sea creatures. He was included in the retinue of his father Poseidon. He made waves in the sea. Many forms of Triton depictions were created after the 4th century BC. Their chests and feet were like those of horses. This way, the three-headed sea monsters that were called the sea centaurs were born. The scariest of these were Scylla and Charybdis.

Thetis

The most famous of the Nereids born from Nereus to Doris were Psamathe, Galatea and Thetis. Among these, Thetis had a special place. Zeus and Poseidon fell in love with Thetis, but as seers knew that the child to be born from her would topple his father from the throne, they both gave up on their love. Unwillingly, they gave Thetis in marriage to Peleus, the king of Thessaly. The marriage of Peleus and Thetis brought forth Achilles, the hero of Greece. Thetis held his son Achilles to fire in order to make him immortal. Arrows would no longer affect the burnt parts of his body, except for his heel where his mother was holding him. Achilles, who killed everyone without being hurt himself, was eventually killed by Paris by being shot on his heel. While trying to make Achilles immortal, Thetis was caught and expelled by Peleus. Already unhappy with her marriage, Thetis began to live with her sisters at the bottom of the sea.

The monument of the Nereids, Xanthos,
400 BC. British Museum.

Uranus and Gaia's son, Hyperion, united with his sister, Thea, and together they brought forth Helios, Selene and Eos. Besides them, there were also celestial and atmospheric deities such as Phaethon, the Harpies and Aeolus. Let us now discuss them briefly.

Helios

He was described as a handsome, strong young man with golden hair. He represented the sun itself, as distinct from god Apollo in Olympus or as a natural power.

Helios first married a nymph named Rhode. He begat a daughter and seven sons from this marriage. His children were known as the Heliades. He married Oceanus's daughter Clymene and begat seven daughters from this marriage. They were known as Helios' daughters. In addition to these girls, he also begat a son named Phaethon from this marriage. Phaethon, whose name means shiny and sparkling, was a frivolous young man. One day, he borrowed the sun chariot from his father Helios. The fiery horses of the chariot noticed that their driver was inexperienced and began to run like crazy. They came so close to the earth that Libya became a desert due to the heat of the sun. Large rivers dried up, and Zeus finally hit the young man with his thunderbolt to save the world from this threat. The legend of Phaethon is best told in Ovid's Metamorphoses.

Helios married Perse of the Titans, the daughter Oceanus and Tethys. From this marriage came forth many children. Circe the magician, Aeetes the king of Colchis, Minoas's wife Pasiaphae and Perses were all their children. Among them Circe and Pasiphae were allowed to practice magic. Helios was shown as a handsome young man with his head surrounded by rays of light in the form of a crown. With his chariot pulled by very fast and fiery horses, he would rise from the east every morning following the dawn and sink into the river of Oceanus every evening. Helios saw everything and was deemed to be the eye of the earth. He saw that Aphrodite and Ares were secretly making love and reported them. White horses, roosters and poplar trees were dedicated to him. The people of Rhodes deemed Helios as the guardian of their cities and thus erected a massive bronze statue of him. This sculpture, which was considered to be one of the Seven

Wonders of the World, remained standing for 80 years. On every corner of the empire, Helios began to be worshipped by the Romans from the 3rd century AD.

Selene

Symbolizing the moon, Selene was born from the marriage of Hyperion and Thea. She was the sister of Helios the god of sun and Eos the goddess of dawn. She was depicted as a beautiful woman touring the skies on a chariot with silver wheels, pulled by two horses. She united with Zeus and gave birth to a daughter named Pandia from him. She united with the god Pan in Arcadia and Pan gave her a herd of white oxen as a gift. The most famous love of Selene, however, was Endymion, who was the shepherd of the mountains of Latmos (Beşparmak) near Lake Bafa in Anatolia.

Eos

Eos, the sister of Helios and Selene, symbolized the dawn. She made the sweet wind of dawn blow and sprinkled drops of dew on plants. Luminous colors would arise where she passed. She was envisioned as an energetic woman having wings on her back and feet, flying with her hair winnowed by the wind. She is described in Homer's Illiad as "the child of morning, rosy-fingered dawn."

The goddess of dawn married Astraeus (the starry heaven) and born from this marriage were the wind gods named Zephyrus, Boreas and Notus. After the winds, the morning star as the harbinger of the day and the stars in the sky were born. One morning, Eos made love to Ares, which was seen and envied by Aphrodite. Therefore, Aphrodite punished Eos by making her constantly fall in love. Eos kidnapped each of her lovers to different places. For instance, she kidnapped Orion the giant to the island of Delos, Cephalus to Syria, and Tithonus, the son of king Laomedon of Troy, to Ethiopia. From the union of Eos with Tithonus came forth Memnon. Having become the king of Ethiopia later, Memnon came to the aid of Troy during the Trojan War and was killed by Achilles. Eos cried every day for the loss of her son and her tears fell on the plants as drops of dew every morning. Eos was sometimes shown as a nymph with flowers around her head and riding the chariot pulled by the winged horse Pegasus. She would hold a torch in her left hand and spread out roses with her right hand. Eos was depicted in the ceiling frescoes of the Baroque period as the harbinger of the day and the goddess who defeated the night.

Embossment of Helios from the Temple of Athena in Troy. 300 BC.

Harpies

Hurricane goddesses Harpies were the daughters of the Oceanid Electra and Thaumas. Their name Harpy means in Greek "that which snatches". Homer only tells of Harpya Podarge the "fleet foot", who united with Zephyrus. Hesiod mostly described two different Harpies. These were Aello (hurricane) and Ocypete (swift flying, gale). The Harpies were described as swift-winged birds with beautiful hair, which raced with birds and winds. These harpies, who had the face of a woman, body of a bird, and sharp claws, were believed to kidnap children and carry the spirits of the dead to Hades. The Harpies Monument in Xanthos has embossments illustrating the Harpies carrying in their arms a spirit swaddled like a baby, to Hades. Harpies are also featured in the story of King Phineas of Thrace as told in the myth of the Argonauts. As one legend has it, Harpies united with Zephyrus the god of wind and formed the immortal horses of Achilles: Xanthos and Balios.

Depiction of the sun god Helios on a vase. 345 BC.

Aeolus

This king of the winds was the son of Poseidon the god of sea. He commanded four great winds which were Notus, Boreos, Euros, and Zephyrus. He would either release them or keep them in a bag, with the order Zeus. He lived on the island of Aeolia together with his six sons and six daughters. He ruled over the winds. As told in the Odyssey, he gave a bag full of fierce winds to Odysseus. He also played an important role in the legend of Aeneas.

Astraeus

He was the husband of Eos the goddess of dawn, and the father of certain stars and winds. Heosphorus and Phosphorus represented the morning star, whereas Hesperus represented the evening star. The sons of Eos and Astraeus all represented the winds; Boreas, the northeast wind, Zephyrus the northwest wind, Euros the east wind, and Notus the southwest wind.

DEITIES RELATED TO HUMAN LIFE AND FATE

Asclepius

Asclepius, the god of health, was the son of Apollo and Coronis. The Roman version of this god of health was worshipped by the adopted name "Aesculapius". One day, the god Apollo lay with Coronis, the daughter of Phlegyas, who was the king of Thessaly. Through this, Coronis became pregnant. She slept with a young man while carrying Apollo's child in her womb. Apollo's sacred bird, the raven, reported this to Apollo.

Apollo was so furious at this that he caused the white feathers of this bird to become jet black. Pindar tells that the god Apollo witnessed the incident in person. Whether or not the news of this situation was given by the bird or the god witnessed this first hand, truly and clearly, Coronis willingly made love to the young man.

Apollo would not allow this betrayal to be left alone and he caused the death of this beautiful woman who had cheated on him. When Coronis was about to be consumed by the flames from the wood stacked upon a pyre, Apollo could not have the heart to kill his own unborn child, so he took the child from her womb and gave the newborn to the centaur Chiron.

Half horse and half man, Chiron was a good being who made medicines from herbs and medicinal plants in nature. Apollo's child, Asclepius was known to have been taught by this master to become a proficient physician. Asclepius progressed day by day through practice, improving his patients and even succeeded in reviving the dead. The goddess Athena also contributed to this event.

When Athena killed the Gorgons, Asclepius gathered their flowing blood. The blood circulating on the right side of a gorgon's body was said to contain toxins, while the blood circulating on the left side of the body was beneficial. The blood of these monsters was useful for Asclepius to revive the dead, but this disrupted the natural order of the gods. Zeus was uncomfortable with this god-like power. Therefore, Asclepius was struck down by a lightning bolt released to the ground. The healer god brought the last medical service to humanity when he died by writing one last prescription. Zeus caused rain and made this prescription melt in the soil.

Sculpture of Asclepius, the god of health, and his son Telesphorus. Roman Period. 2nd century AD. İstanbul Archaeology Museums.

Outlook from the Asclepeion in Pergamum

Soon, a plant began to emerge from the ground as a panacea, which is claimed to be the garlic plant. The last gift of the physician god to the people became the garlic plant. Asclepius' constellations were formed in the sky after his death had taken place.

Apollo was very sad at his son's death, but could not do anything to the chief god, Zeus, but took revenge against Zeus by killing of the Cyclopes who gave Zeus his thunderbolts. Asclepius' medicine was continued by his sons, who were known as the Asclepiads, and by his daughter Hygieia. The snake is accepted to be his symbol, and he was sometimes depicted while presenting a glass of drink to a snake hanging from his neck. Today, doctors use this snake as their symbol. Many physicians, such as Hippocrates of Cos, are considered to be the sons of Asclepius.

Temples

The temples of the god Asclepius were known as Asclepeion. The most important temples of the physician god were located in Epidaurus and Cos (İstanköy), Greece. The most widely established Asclepeion in Anatolia was located in Pergamum. Excavations revealed that this temple

existed in the 4th century BC, developed during the Hellenistic era, and lived its heyday during the 2nd century AD.

The Roman Asclepeion was 820 m. in length, and 18.14 m. in width, and was accessed via a colonnaded sacred way. It covered an area of 130 x 110 m. surrounded by columns on three sides. This place offered a wide range of spa treatment for patients including Asclepeion music, psychological guidance and culture, which were all utilized as instruments for treatment. Today, the 3500-seat theater here has been restored. Across from here, the Asclepius Temple, which was built in AD150 by the Consul L. Cuspius Pactumeius Rufinus, can be seen. This temple was built to represent a small scale of the Pantheon in Rome which was built two decades earlier.

Besides this, there was also a circular building with six apses for medical treatment. This building connected to the other treatment buildings through a tunnel. Patients were treated in these tunnels, which have been uncovered today. Water and the music were heard in the tunnel. This was the most effective treatment in the Asclepeion at Pergamum, besides mud baths. The way people were treated at the Asclepeion in the 2nd century AD was explained by the orator Aelius Aristeides, who stayed there for thirteen years around the mid-2nd century. Patients were treated by spiritual guidance during their sleep, and there were sleeping rooms for this purpose. Psychiatric patients were also treated in the theater with music.

The holy water in the pool, which has radioactive properties according to recent studies, was used to offer physical therapy to patients, who were also treated in the tunnels and sleeping rooms by guidance. The best and brightest of the doctors of the time, such as Galenus and Satyrus, lived, worked and taught during the heydays of the Asclepeion. Asclepius lived in the Asclepeion of Pergamum, together with his daughter Hygieia. The cult of Telesphorus, who lived before his time, was still being practiced then. The statues of Asclepius are typically old and bearded, and show him wearing a laurel crown. Additionally, they are seen holding a staff with a serpent wrapped around it. His other symbols besides snake were pine cones, laurel wreaths, and sometimes a goat or a dog.

Moirae (Parcae)

Hesiod defines the Moirae as *"those who organize the shares of our life"*. The Moirae, in other words the goddesses of fate, were the three sisters born in the marriage of Zeus and Themis. Clotho spun the thread of life, Lachesis was the personification of destiny, and Atropos applied the inevitable, unchangeable fate that was decided. Even Zeus could not change her decision. According to the old belief, man's destiny was decided in the womb. Then the destiny began to spin the thread of life. The three Moerae kept spinning the yarn of every man, and one day the yarn would be twisted and cut off. The fates of people were engraved on iron and bronze in the palace of the goddesses and nothing could erase them. The symbol of Clotho, who spun the thread of human life, was a roller spinner. The roll of paper and spheres were the symbols of Lachesis who determined the length of life. The scissors and scales were the symbols of Atropos.

Nemesis

According to Hesiod, Nemesis, the goddess of jealousy and revenge, was the daughter of the goddess of the night, Nyx. Human ignorance, excessive pride, confidence and ebullience of luck to the extreme were punished by her. Zeus admired Nemesis, but his feelings were not reciprocated by her. Nemesis would enter into various forms to escape Zeus. However, when Nemesis transformed into a goose, Zeus took the form of a swan and lay with her and impregnated her. Nemesis was told to have produced eggs which were taken by Leda, after this relationship.

Statue of Nemesis, the goddess of divine justice. 2nd century AD. Burdur Museum.

Helen and the Dioscuri were hatched from these eggs. Nemesis, symbolizing divine anger, is often confused with the Erinyes. She was mostly depicted as the being who punished the excess of people, excessive confidence in self and fortune. She came after the god of delusion, Ate, and the god of insolence, Hybris. In arts, she was illustrated as a serious and thoughtful girl. When representing moderation, Nemesis was shown with a ruler, or with her finger on her lips. When representing punishment, she was illustrated with a belt or a sword. Sometimes she was illustrated in the chariot pulled by the Griffins. In a small town of Attica, near Marathon, there was a small temple for Nemesis. The statue of Nemesis inside the temple was said to be the work of the famous sculptor Phidias. Beautiful statues of Nemesis can be seen in the Burdur Museum and İstanbul Archeology Museums.

Tyche (Fortuna)

Tyche was one of the daughters of Oceanus and Tethys and was the goddess of fate and fortune. However, she was not the personification of bad fate like the Moerae. She symbolized bright fortune, happiness and success. Tyche was also the symbol of independence. She was very popular in Rome with the name Fortuna. She held a cornucopia in her hand or a ship wheel. She was sometimes depicted as rolling over a sphere and having wings. Ancient Greeks used the phrase "Agathe Tykhe" to wish "Good luck". Fortuna, which was an ancient cult in the Latium region of Italy, became identical with the Tyche of the Greeks after the 1st century BC. Tyche was also used in Latin. In sculptures, she was shown while holding a cornucopia in her hand and wearing a crown made of city walls.

Generally, she was depicted with a ship wheel or cornucopia. Sphere and the wings symbolized changeability. There are beautiful statues of Tyche, like the one in the İstanbul Archaeology Museums, in addition to some foreign museums. The statue which was found in Düzce, was inspired by the statues of Tyche from the 4th century BC. She is wearing a crown decorated with olive leaves and representing the city walls. In her left arm, she is holding a cornucopia filled with various fruits, while at the same time carrying the child named Plutus, who was the embodiment of prosperity. There is a statue of Tyche on Mount Nemrut, besides those of the gods such as Zeus and Apollo. The chief god of the city of Antiocheia founded by the Seleucids was also Tyche.

Statue of Tyche, Roman-era copy of a 4th century BC work.
İstanbul Archaeology Museums.

WOODLAND AND RURAL DEITIES

Woodland and rural deities were creatures such as Oreads, Auloniads, Dryads and Nymphs. Oreads were "mountain nymphs", Auloniads were "nymphs of glens," and Dryads' were "nymphs of trees' which they protected. Let us also give some information about Echo, an Oread, Nymphs, who were woodland spirits, and Silenus and Satyrs.

Satyrs

Satyrs and sileni were spirits which symbolized nature. The upper part of their body was humanlike while the other part of their body was sometimes seen as a horse and sometimes as a goat. Their feet were shaped as goat's feet. They wandered around the moorlands, tagged along behind the Maenads and Nymphs while chasing them. Mainly, they took part in the affairs of Dionysus and Pan. Satyrs were mostly animated in plastic arts and paintings. Marsyas, who challenged Apollo in a musical contest, was also a satyr.

Old satyrs were generally known as the sileni. The first satyrs were told to be the children of Dionysus and the naiad nymph Nicaea. It is also believed that they also used to be humans. As they made Hera angry, she gave them goat horns and goat feet as punishment. Aegipans were hairy creatures which descended from the same ancestors. The Satyr sculpture made by Praxiteles around 350 BC was very famous. A copy of it from the Roman period is kept in the Capitolium Museum of Rome. An enormous sculpture of the 'sleeping Satry' can be seen in the Glyptothek Museum in Munich. Also, Jupiter's approaching Antiope in appearance as a Satyr was demonstrated pithily on a canvas by the artist Tiziano.

Silenus

In the beginning, Silenus, a rustic deity from Phrygia, was shown as a bald, old man with a large stomach. He was a child born either to Pan or Hermes by a Nymph. As he was always drunk, he walked with the help of Satyrs. Sometimes he rode a donkey but he always fell down. Silenus had animal ears and a tail. He was always seen in the retinue of Dionysus.

The members of the Orpheus cult, also known as the Orphics, later developed this Anatolian-originating and primitive-looking Silenus.

Statue of Silenus holding the child Dionysus in his arms.

Mosaic of the dancing Maenad and Satyr. Roman Period. Antakya Museum.

According to this, Silenus was accepted as an old, wise man who had the ability of foresight. From this aspect, he trained the Anatolian-originating Dionysus. It is seen that one Silenus later became several sileni. They were the inventors of musical instruments. In art and literature, they were frequently confused with Satyrs. We come across two types of Satyrs in sculptures, one representing the trainer Silenus who holds the child Dionysus in his arms, and the other the intoxicated Silenus who wears a wreath of climber and vine leaves. He is mentioned in the poems of Virgil and Plato's dialogue 'Symposium'.

Centaurs

Centaurs were creatures known as 'horse men' in mythology as their body was half human and half horse. They were the children of Ixion, king of the Lapiths and Nephele. When seen from the front side, their chest and head

were humanlike and their body was horse-like. Sometimes their arms and legs were shaped as a human. These mountain-dwelling horsemen, who ate raw meat, were wild creatures. Some of them were benevolent and some of them were evil. For example, Chiron, who taught the art of medicine to the god of medicine, Asclepius, was a good Centaur. Chiron did not descend from the same family as the other Centaurs. He was the son of Cronus and Philyra. Pholus, who was born to Silenus and to Melia, an ash tree nymph, was a well-mannered and hospitable Centaur. For example, while Heracles was on the way to hunt Erymanthian boar, he became the guest of Pholus. The Lapith king Pirithous was going to marry Hippodameia, the daughter of Oenomaus the king of Argos. Heracles, Theseus and Centaurs were also invited. During the wedding, the Centaurs started to molest the bride with the effect of alcohol, going to extremes and trying to kidnap the bride, for which reason a fight between the Lapiths and Centaurs occurred. With the help of Heracles and Theseus, they chased the Centaurs to the mountains. The surviving

Centaurs managed to take shelter on the islands where the Sirens lived, but they all eventually died there. This fight has been dramatically taken up by numerous poets, artists and painters. In the following periods, the Centaurs were described as creatures having upper human bodies arising from a horse body. For example, it is possible to see this in the embossments in the Parthenon which were created by Phidias.

Lapiths

The Lapiths were a Thessallian clan, which is mentioned both in legends and in history. The ancestor of the Lapiths is told to be the river god Peneus. Peneus married Creusa and they had a son and a daughter. Their daughter became pregnant from Apollo and gave birth to a son named Lapithes. He gave his name to the lineage of the Lapiths. They are also described in the Iliad.

Pan

The son of Hermes, Pan was the god of the shepherds. He was a goat-footed and double horned god who liked to dance with nymphs gaily in the moorlands. He played the shepherd's pipe well and made beautiful melodies with his pipe. The nymphs would surround Pan, who would wear a red lynx pelt, sang complimentary songs to him. After indulging in his siesta, Pan would like to appear suddenly in front of travelers in solitude, and scare them. He protected the herds and shepherds and he symbolized abundance. Pan pursued Syrinx, the daughter of Ladon, but the nymph did not comply with his requests. She begged the gods to protect her and they turned her into a reed. Pan became disappointed, so he cut seven reeds and made his shepherd's pipe. Afterwards, this instrument became the most prominent sign of the god. Pan's counterpart in Latin Mythology is Faunus.

Echo

Echo, who was a mountain nymph, was playful and chatty. While Zeus consorted with the mountain and woodland nymphs, she distracted the attention of Hera and hindered her from watching his husband. One day, Hera realized this trick and punished Echo by making her repeat every word she heard.

Another legend has it that, Echo was being consumed by the love of Narcissus, her body turned into a rock and only her voice remained. According to another legend, as Echo was not indulgent with Pan, she incurred the wrath of Pan and was ruptured by shepherds.

Group sculpture of Aphrodite, Eros and Pan. 2nd century BC.

Hades

The son of Cronus and Rhea, Hades was the brother of Zeus. Before Zeus began to reign in Olympus, he divided the universe among his brothers. Zeus took Olympus and the sky, Poseidon took the seas, and the underworld fell to Hades. Thus, Hades became the god of the land of the dead. Known as Pluto in Latin, Hades also had the ability to be invisible. What made this god invisible was his helmet. From time to time, Athena, Hermes, Perseus and Heracles wore the same helmet. Hades stole Persephone, the daughter of Demeter. Upon the pleadings of Demeter, who could not bear this pain, Zeus persuaded Hades to allow Persephone to stay with her mother for six months. When Persephone came back to the surface, she would revitalize nature, bringing along spring and summer. When she returned to Hades, all of the trees would die from sadness, shedding their leaves, which turned yellow, and the winter would come. Hades's dog Cerberus guarded the door to the land of the dead and would bite whoever attempted to go out. Styx was the underground river. Although Hades was generally faithful to his wife, he had a relationship with a naiad nymph named Minthe. When Persephone found out, she turned Minthe into a mint plant. He also had a relationship with Oceanus's daughter Leuce, which resulted in her being transformed into a silver poplar tree.

Erinyes

The Erinyes were the merciless goddesses of hell punishing whoever violated or challenged the moral order. According to Hesiod, they were born of the blood coming from the castrated genitals of Uranus. They were the goddesses of vengeance. These three women were named Alecto, Tisiphone and Megaera. Erinyes were generally envisioned as dragons chasing after criminals, mostly murderers. These female dragons would drive the criminals they pursued insane by chasing them forever, following their smell of blood. The snake was their immutable sign. In his "Eumenides", Aeschylus describes them as female dragons having snakes for hair like gorgons. In

Sculpture of the god Hades from the Roman Period. It was found at the theater of Hierapolis. End of the 2nd century AD. Pamukkale Museum.

Vase illustrating Heracles and Cerberus, the hell hound. 530 BC.

"Orestes", Euripides describes Erinyes as winged and snake-haired girls pursuing criminals with torches. Through time, Erinyes were seen as goddesses who punished people underground. Appearing in the old texts, this belief also recurs in Virgil's epic of Aeneid, in which Erinyes are depicted while torturing spirits with the snakes and whips in their hands. They are illustrated in the same way in plastic arts as well. Sometimes torches are replaced by whips, arrows and quivers.

Hypnos (Sleep) and Thanatos (Death)

These two brothers were the children of Nyx, the night goddess. These brothers, who were always side by side and lived in the depths of Tartarus under the ground. Thanatos was the personification of the inevitable and silent dead. Thus he was shaped as a winged spirit. He was also shown as a sleeping child or as a young boy. In time, his

Hades and Demeter figure on a vase dating approximately to 430 BC.

sign became a torch, burning or extinguished. Hypnos is seen in different forms. He was depicted as eagle-winged or with a butterfly on the forehead. He was also shown while holding a poppy stalk in his hand or with a horn. According to a legend, Hypnos fell in love with Endymion, the shepherd of Mount Latmus, and enabled him to sleep with his eyes open so that he could admire his beloved to his heart's content.

Oneiroi (Dream)

Dreams were considered as the children of sleep by poets. From these, the one taking a human form was known as Morpheus, the one with animal appearance was named Icelus, and the one taking the form of inanimate objects was known as Phantasos. In arts, the Oneiroi were demonstrated either alone or together with Hypnos.

There are many famous lineages in mythology, and many well-known heroes descending from them. For instance, Theseus is of sacred Athenian lineage, Achilles is of the Aeacids, Oedipus is of the lineage of Cadmus, and Agamemnon, Menelaus and Aias are of the lineage of Tantalus. There is also the lineage of Atlas. Oceanus's daughter Pleione gave seven daughters to Atlas. Taygete, who was one of these daughters, known as the Pleiades, made love to Zeus and bare a son named Lacedaemon. Perieres, who came from the lineage of Lacedaemon, married the daughter of Perseus and Andromeda. From this marriage four sons came forth as Aphareus, Leucippus, Ikarius and Tyndareus. Let us now talk about the lineages of Aeacus and Pelops. Zeus and Aegina, the daughter of the river god Asopus, had a son named Aeacus. Aeacus wished from Zeus that the ants on the island of Aegina became human beings. Zeus granted his wish and transformed the ants on the island into human beings. Aeacus, who was a wise man, married the daughter of Chiron. From this marriage, Achilles's father Peleus and Aias the Great's father Telamon were born. His second wife, Psamathe, bare him Phocus. The famous wedding of Peleus and Thetis, daughter of Nereus, brought about many incidents, which we already talked about. While discussing Thetis, we learned how Achilles was rendered half immortal by his mother Thetis. The story of Achilles will be given in the section about Troy. Telamon's son, Aias, participated in the Calydonian hunt and the voyage of the Argonauts. Together with Heracles, he participated in another expedition before the Trojan war. Telamon married Hesione, the daughter of King Laomedon of Troy. This marriage brought forth Teucer. Let us now discuss these heroes starting with Agamemnon.

Agamemnon - Menelaus

Chief Commander of the Trojan War and king of kings, Agamemnon faced an intriguing fate. His ancestors can be traced back to Tantalus. Tantalus was the son of Zeus and Pluto. This child of the gods, Tantalus was king of Lydia. He reigned in Mount Sipylus near Manisa. He was wealthy and powerful. He had a son name Pelops and a daughter named

Vase illustration of the wedding of Achilles's father Peleus and the goddess Thetis. 340 BC.

Niobe. Because he had a different religion and culture, this king was cursed by the Olympian gods. His bragging and the fact that he cut his son Pelops into pieces and attempted to feed him to the gods caused him to be severely punished in hell after his death.

Zeus resurrected Pelops after he was killed by his father. Later, Pelops went to Greece, where he participated in contests and triumphed. This triumph enabled him to marry Hippodameia, daughter of king Oenomaus. After a while, he went back to his homeland together with his wife. Pelops and Hippodameia had six sons and three daughters. The most famous of their sons were Atreus, Thyestes, Alcathous and Pittheus. Atreus had a sorrowful life which was featured in tragedies. Atreus, the father of Agamemnon, was of a cursed lineage. Therefore, he underwent many ordeals. Atreus and Thyestes killed their step-brother, who was born to their father Pelops and a nymph. Thus, Pelops cursed and expelled his two sons. Atreus and his brother Thyestes took refuge behind the king of Mycenae. After a while, the king died and his successor subsequently died, too, without being able to assign a successor. The Oracles advised the people of Mycenae to elect one of the sons of Pelops as their king. This situation brought the two brothers in enmity. Each of them engaged in various plots to do away with the other. Atreus possessed a flock of sheep and one of these had a golden fleece – the symbol of royal power. Despite having promised to do so, Atreus failed to sacrifice this sheep to Artemis. Instead, he kept the fleece to himself. Thyestes took hold of this fleece by seducing Atreus's wife Aerope. Whoever had the golden fleece would become the king.

However, Zeus helped Atreus to secure the throne. Atreus ascended to the throne and expelled his brother from Mycenae. When he found out that he and his wife betrayed him, however, he recalled him to his palace. He killed the three children of Thyestes, had their meat cooked, and served his brother this food made from his own children. Later, he showed his brother the cut-off heads of the children. After this incident, Thyestes left the place denouncing what happened. This obscene situation embarrassed the sun too, which in return hid itself bringing everything to darkness.

Thyestes took shelter in Sicyon. Unknowingly, he married his own daughter Pelopeia. This union produced a child named Aegisthus. This child and his mother later came to the palace of Atreus. Atreus married this woman and adopted the child. When the child grew up, Atreus ordered him to kill Thyestes. Yet, Aegisthus discovered the truth and killed Atreus instead of his own father. Atreus had two sons from his wife Aerope. These were Agamemnon and Menelaus. When Atreus died, Thyestes became the king and expelled Atreus's sons Agamemnon and Menelaus to Mycenae. They took shelter in the palace of the Spartan king.

King Tyndareus of Sparta reigned here, together with his wife Leda. One day, while his wife Leda was bathing in the lake, Zeus approached her disguising himself as a swan. They united and created two eggs. One of these eggs had Helen and Polydeuces in it, while the other one had Castor and Clytemnestra. Helen and Polydeuces were assumed to be of Zeus, while Castor and Clytemnestra were assumed to be of King Tyndareus.

These children were grown up when Agamemnon and Menelaus came to the palace of Sparta. The girls were of marriage age. Castor was skilled at horseback riding, and Polydeuces was a good fighter. They were known as "Dioscuri" meaning the sons of Zeus. Menelaus married Helen, and Agamemnon married Clytemnestra. At the time the throne was vacated in the kingdom of Mycenae, so Agamemnon went back to Mycenae and assumed the throne. He became the most powerful king in Greece. He and his wife Clytemnestra had children named Iphigenia, Chrysothemis, Electra and Orestes. Aegisthus is known to have taken the throne of Agamemnon while he was in Troy. Aegisthus and Clytemnestra killed Agamemnon when he came back from Troy.

Meleager

Meleager was the son of Althaea, and the sister of Leda and Oeneus, king of Calydon in Aetolia. In one harvesting season, Oeneus offered sacrifices to all of the gods but forgot about Artemis. Artemis was outraged by his forgetfulness and thus released a large boar to the region of Calydon and had it eat the crops. The boar ate everything that it came across. Therefore, a famine and drought broke out in the region. To get rid of this beast, the king called heroes from Greece for help. He promised that he would give the skin of the boar to whoever killed it. Many heroes arrived to participate in this hunt for the Calydonian boar. The neighboring Curetes also came to take part in this hunt. The king hosted his guests for nine days and finally, the hunting began. Even though the boar killed some of the hunters, it was finally besieged, and a beautiful huntress Atalanta from Arcadia shot it with an arrow on its back. Then, Meleager killed it by thrusting his spear into its stomach. He peeled the skin of the boar and gave it to Atalanta as a gift. However, Artemis's grudge had not passed. She instilled a fight this time, between the Aetolians and their neighbors, over the sharing of the prey. The hunters fell out with each other, and during this fight, Meleager killed his uncles. Thereupon, his mother Althaea uttered curses against her son. Meleager withdrew from the fight in sorrow. The Curetes ravaged the cities of Aetolians. All of his friends pleaded with Meleager, thus he could not resist these pleas and returned to the war and dismissed the Curetes from Calydon.

There is another account of the legend of Meleager. When Meleager was little, oracles told his mother that he would die when the log in the furnace was burnt to the ground. Therefore, Meleager's mother took the log that was burning in the furnace and hid it. When her son killed his uncles during the hunting of the Calydonian boar, she was outraged and took out the log where it was hiding and threw it into the furnace. When the log was burnt to the ground, Meleager's life came to an end. Upon the death of Meleager, his mother went through a crisis and hanged herself. Meleager's wife, too, killed herself.

Meleager, the personification of a fearless hero, was depicted by artists as a strong and handsome young man. His depictions show him while leaning on a spear, with a sullen face. The legend of Meleager was excellently featured on a sarcophagus dating to the 2nd century AD, which is in the İstanbul Archaeology Museums.

Orpheus

Orpheus was reportedly the son of the muse Calliope, and either King Oeagrus of Thrace or the god Apollo. Orpheus is the first known bard of antiquity. He played his lyre excellently and calmed the animals with his music. Even trees were enchanted by the music he played.

Orpheus fell in love with Eurydice, the oak nymph, and married her. However, his wife Eurydice was killed by a snake bite, while trying to flee Aristaeus, an adept beekeeper and hunter who always pursued her. Orpheus went down to Hades to bring his wife back from the land of the dead. He mesmerized Hades, the god of the underworld, and his wife Persephone, with his amazing music. They allowed his wife to return to the earth, lest this great musician suffer. Still, they told Orpheus not to look back at the face of his wife until they climbed up to the earth. Before long, Orpheus forgot about this rule and could not help but look at his beloved wife's face. Thus he lost her completely and returned to his homeland, Thrace. He is told to have been foraged by the frenzy Maenads there. Muses collected the pieces of Orpheus and buried them in Pieria. It is believed that the head and lyre of Orpheus, which were thrown into a river, reached the sea and landed on the island of Lesbos (Midilli). The fact that the island of Lesbos raised many bards is attributed to this event. Virgil, the Latin poet, told of Orpheus in his Georgica. In the antiquity, a mystical religion named Orphism appeared which was associated with Orpheus. Orpheus was pointed out as the founder of this religion. There is an exquisite mosaic of Orpheus in Antakya Museum today.

Perseus

As mentioned before, in the section about Zeus, King Acrisius learned that he was going to be killed by the child to be born of his daughter. Therefore, he did not allow his daughter Danae to meet anybody and kept her in a bronze chamber. Zeus entered into this chamber in the form of a golden rain drop and impregnated Danae. When Danae was due, she gave birth to a child named Perseus. This worried the king; therefore, he placed his daughter and grandson into a boat and let it float in the sea. Zeus knew everything; he helped the mother and son to step on the island of Seriphus. Diktys, who was the brother of King Polydectes, found them on the shore.

Time went by and Perseus grew up. In the meantime, King Polydectes fell in love with Danae. But his son Perseus was in his way. To do away with him, he gave Perseus an order to bring the head of the Gorgon Medusa. Believing that he will be unable to succeed in such a grand task, Perseus asked Athena and Hermes for help and they accepted.

The gods took Perseus to the Graiae, who were a trilogy of hags guarding the Gorgons. These hags had only a single eye and a tooth which they alternately used. These three hags were the only ones to know how to reach the nymphs who hid the three must-haves that would allow Perseus to accomplish his duty. When the Graiae refused to tell Perseus what he asked for, he took the single eye and tooth that they used jointly. Therefore, they had to give Perseus the information he needed in return for their eye and tooth.

Perseus went to the nymphs and took from them the winged sandals, Hades's invisibility hat and the magic sack called the kibisis, all of which were indispensable to kill Medusa. Hermes also gave Perseus a diamond sickle. Athena gave him a mirror. Perseus flew on his winged sandals and headed for Oceanus. There he found the three Gorgons. These

Overleaf: Orpheus Mosaic. 8 x 7 m. Antakya Museum.

Mosaic showing Andromeda and Perseus. Roman Period. Antakya Museum.

creatures, with snake's hair, boar's teeth, bronze hands and golden wings, would transform their onlookers into a stone. Of these three Gorgons, only Medusa was mortal. Perseus did not look at Medusa and approached her walking backwards. With the help of the mirror Athena gave him, and the diamond sickle, he cut off the head of Medusa. Blood running from her slain head brought forth Chrysaor and the winged horse Pegasus.

Perseus put the slain head of Gorgon into a sack and left the place flying. Meanwhile, Medusa's two sisters woke and discovered that their sister was killed, and began pursuing Perseus. However, they lost track of Perseus because he wore the invisibility hat of Hades.

Perseus reached Ethiopia flying over many lands. Here, Cassiopeia, who was the wife of King Cepheus, prided herself on her beauty so much. This was to such an extent that she even claimed that she was more beautiful than the daughters of Nereus. Therefore, the Nereids asked Poseidon for help to cut her down to size. Poseidon could not refuse the

wish of the Nereids and sent a dragon to Ethiopia. The dragon destroyed everything in Ethiopia that came across him. The king consulted with soothsayers to eradicate this dragon. The soothsayers let the king know that his daughter Andromeda would have to be sacrificed to get rid of this plight. Hence, they tied Andromeda on a rock and began waiting for the dragon to arrive. Around this time, Perseus happened to be in Ethiopia, passing by. He saw this outstandingly beautiful girl tied onto a rock, waiting to be the prey of the dragon. He fell in love with this helpless girl at first sight. He untied the girl and slain the dragon with his diamond sickle. Therefore, he was declared the savior of the country and married Andromeda. However, Andromeda had been engaged to somebody else. Her fiancé attempted to kill this new lover in an ambush, but Perseus showed the head of Medusa to him and turned him into a stone. Finally, Perseus took Andromeda with him and returned to Seriphus. There, King Polydectes would take his hands off his mother Danae. Perseus showed the head of Medusa to the king and transformed him into stone as well. Later, he made Diktys king, who had found them on the shore. He gave the head of Medusa to Athena, who had this head crafted on to her breastplate as a decoration. He gave the winged sandals and the invisibility hat to Hermes and returned to Argos. His grandfather Acrisius, King of Argos, had left his country to overturn the prophecy that his daughter's child would kill him. He settled in the city of Larissa Thessaly.

After a while, Perseus set off to join the races organized in Larissa. Thus the fate was sealed; Perseus participated in the race there and the discus he threw hit and killed his grandfather. Perseus, deeply upset by this, relinquished the throne of Argos. He left the throne in Argos to Megapenthes, who was his kin, and he took the throne in Tiryns. Perseus's depictions reflect his experiences. Medusa is also seen on the embossments.

Argonauts

Let us now explore the Argo sailors, or in other words, the Argonauts which is one of the legendary stories of antiquity – because it relates to Anatolia as well. The ship Argo was a 50-oar ship which was built for the heroes of Colchis in their quest to find the golden fleece. The voyage was named as Argonauts after the builder of it. King Aeson of Iolcus lost his throne to his step-brother Pelias. Aeson's little son survived the massacre that took place and was raised in a remote land. When he was of age, he reclaimed the throne of his father from King Pelias. Oracles advised the king to be wary of a person with a single foot. To get rid of him, Pelias asked him to go to Colchis and bring the golden fleece which Phrixus had left there. Let us continue our story by explaining why and how this golden fleece went there. King Athamas grew tired of his wife Nephele and chose Ino as his second wife. Nephele feared that her children Helle and Phrixus would be harmed by Ino, the new wife of the king. This is because Ino planned to have her step-son Phrixus killed and her own son to replace King Athamas on the throne. Ino began to put her evil plans into action one by one. First, she dried the seeds, which caused a famine in the country that year. The king sent a harbinger to the temple, inquiring what needed to be done. The wicked queen took control of the harbinger and made him advise the king that he had to sacrifice Phrixus, his son from his ex-wife, to eradicate the famine. The king accepted to sacrifice his son to save his people from the famine. When the child was about to be sacrificed, the gods could not resist the implorations of his father and sent a ram with golden

Vase illustration depicting the finding of the golden fleece. 350-340 BC. Louvre Müzesi.

fleece from heaven. This ram picked Phrixus and his sister Helle, and flew away. It dropped Helle while flying over the Dardanelles Strait. Ever since that day, the Dardanelles Strait came to be called Hellespontos meaning the sea of Helle. The ram with golden fleece took Phrixus to the land of Colchis (Georgia) by the Black Sea. In the meantime, Phrixus sacrificed the ram with golden fleece to Zeus and gave the fleece to King Aeetes. He kept this fleece in the forest of Ares.

This is the story of the golden fleece which the king asked Jason to bring. Argos, the ship builder, Tiphys the helmsman; Mopsus, Amphiaraus and Idmon who were the famous seers of that age, together with Peleus, Telamon, famous bard Orpheus, in addition to many heroes such as Meleager and Heracles joined this voyage upon the request of Jason.

The Argo ship set sail from a port in Thessaly. The first stop of the Argonauts was the island of Lemnos. There, the women had no men because they had killed their husbands. Thus they welcomed the Argonauts. They made love to them and became pregnant. Later, the Argonauts went on sailing and reached the island of Samothrace (Semendirek) before arriving at the Dardanelles Strait. They moved on from there to the Sea of Marmara, arriving in Cyzicus on the Kapıdağ Peninsula. This was the land of the Delionians. They were welcome there too. After they set sail from that town, a storm broke and the Argonauts had to return. The Delionians thought that pirates were raging their city and began to fight these newcomers in the darkness of the night. A fierce war was waged between them and King Cyzikus of the Delionians was killed by Jason. Then came the morning and the misunderstanding became clear; the Argonauts mourned over the death of King Cyzikus for three days and nights. Afterwards, the Argonauts managed to stop the storm by erecting a statue of Cybele on the peninsula of Kapıdağ.

They left this place and came to the shores of Mysia. Probably on the shores of Mudanya, Heracles went into the wilderness to replace the broken oar. He was accompanied by Hylas, who was a young man Heracles liked very much. This young man became lost in the wilderness, and Heracles searched for him until the morning. The Argonauts abandoned hope on Heracles and Hylas, and thus sailed off and continued their journey.

When the Argonauts came to what is called the Asian shores of İstanbul today, they encountered the giant Amykos there. Polydeuces defeated the giant and they set sail again. However, there was a storm, which drifted the ship of the Argonauts to the coast of Thrace. There they met the blind king Phineus, son of Poseidon. This king was troubled by the Harpies, who were winged monsters with a woman's face. The Harpies were beaten and banished by Calais and Zetes, the sons of the wind god Boreas. In return for this favor, the blind king Phineus informed the Argonauts on how to overcome the dangers that they will face in the future. King Phineus explained how they could pass through the clashing rocks of Symplegades, before they could sail into the Black Sea. These rocks, also known as the blue rocks, would clash together and destroy the ships that attempted to sail through them. Following the advice of Phineus, the sailors first let a dove fly through the rocks. The dove managed to pass at the expense of losing some of its feathers, and so did the ship of Argo with a little damage on its stern. After that day it was told that the clashing rocks became stuck and could never move again. Thus the Argonauts escaped the pernicious streams of the Bosphorus and sailed into the Black Sea. Their first stop on the Black Sea was the land of the Mariandyni near Sinop. King Lycus welcomed them warmly. During a boar hunting here, Idmon the seer and Tiphys the helmsman died. The Argonauts left this location and reached the land of the Amazons. They did not stay very long in the land of Amazons, which is assumed to have been located near the Terme River by the Black Sea, but travelled towards the coasts which viewed the Caucasus Mountains.

They reached the land of Colchis and demanded the golden fleece from King Aeetes. The king's daughter Medea, who happened to be near her father during that time, saw and fell in love with Jason. This girl was at the same time a powerful sorcerer. She helped Jason in carrying out the tasks required by the king. In the end, the Argonauts managed to return taking the golden fleece and the daughter of the king. There were many incidents during their return trip as well. While they were passing by the island of the Sirens, Orpheus put a spell on them with his music so that they could not enchant the sailors. They stopped by Libya and Crete as well, finally arriving in Greece after 4 months. Jason gave the golden fleece to the king and wanted the throne. However, the king did not honor his promise and refused to give the throne. Then the sorcerer Medea came into play. She told the daughters of the king to place their father into the cauldron full of a curative mixture, to render him young again. And she gave them an example: She threw a ram into the cauldron and turned that into a lamb. The daughters of the king believed in this, killed their father and put him in a cauldron full of the mixture. They turned mad seeing that their father did not revive again.

This gruesome event secured the throne for Jason; however, they were expelled due to this homicide. Jason and his sorcerer wife Medea took refuge in Corinth. They lived happily there for ten years. Later, Jason decided to divorce his wife Medea and marry the daughter of the king, Creusa.

Medea gave the bride a poisonous robe as a wedding gift. The new bride died in pain after wearing this piece of clothing which she greatly admired. Next, Medea suffocated his two sons from Jason before his eyes. Later, she left that place and came to Athens and married King Aegeus. She attempted to kill Theseus and was expelled from Athens and thus returned to Colchis. After wandering in misery and starving for a while, Jason committed suicide.

The story of the Argonauts was written by Apollonius of Rhodes who lived in the 3rd century BC. Their story in Greece was written by Euripides.

Theseus

Theseus was the son of King Aegeus of Athens and Aethra. His natural father was told to be Poseidon. Theseus's childhood was spent near his grandfather Pittheus in Troezen. He grew into a young man there, without knowing that he was the son of the king of Athens. The king said to his wife "if you ever bear a son, place a sword and sandals beneath a rock, and show him this when he comes of age to lift the rock". He also advised her, "He shall put on that sword and come near me then, but do not tell him who he is until that time".

At age sixteen, his mother took Theseus to where that rock was located and told him what his husband had said. Theseus lifted the rock and took the sword and sandals beneath it. He put on the sword and wore the sandals. He understood that he was the son of a king and decided to go to Athens to find his father. Theseus encountered many monsters and thieves on the way to Athens. He went on his way killing them one by one. One of the thieves was Sinis, who was known as "Pine-Bender" in the area of the Corinth Strait. He would tie the traveler he caught to a pine tree from his feet, bend the branches and then release them. Then the body of the traveler would split from his legs. Theseus had to deal with this thief first.

Statue of Theseus and the Amazon queen Antiope. 500-490 BC.

After killing him, Theseus went on and encountered a second thief who was named Skiron. He would catch a traveler, make them wash his feet and then throw them into the sea with a kick. Theseus threw him into the sea and thus cleared this part of the road from the thieves. When he arrived at the Crommyon Plain, he killed a wild sow named Phaea. Next, he entered the zone of another thief named Procrustes. This thief would catch travelers, make them lie on a bed, and if the feet of the traveler would extend over the edge of the bed, he would cut them off with a saw. If they were shorter than the bed, he would make them longer by beating them with a hammer. Having overcome his thief as well, Theseus cleaned himself in the river of Cephissus and arrived at the palace of his father. Around that time, the king lived together with the sorcerer named Medea. The sorcerer immediately discerned who the newcomer was. She convinced the king that he was somebody after the throne. Not knowing that this newcomer was his own son, the king cooperated with the sorcerer to hatch a plot to kill him. They asked Theseus to kill the bull of Marathon. Theseus killed the bull and returned to the palace. Medea started looking for other means to kill him and decided to poison him. She held a banquet and extended a glass with poison to Theseus. Before drinking from the glass, Theseus took out his sword to cut the meat. His father recognized the sword and discovered that sitting across from him was his own son and smashed the glass which was full of poison. He embraced his son and expelled the sorcerer Medea from the palace.

Days went by, and it was time for sending the monster of Crete, Minotaur, seven maidens and seven boys. This was an obligation that had to be fulfilled every year. Theseus boarded a ship with large sails, together with the youth from Athens, to go to Crete. He said he would hang a white flag to the ship if he was able to return safely from Crete. When he arrived in Crete, he fell in love with Ariadne, who was the beautiful daughter of King Minos. She told Theseus that she would tell him how to kill the monster if he married her and took her to Athens. The monster lived in a cave that had many paths in it and was impossible to get out. Ariadne gave Theseus a ball of yarn and advised him to tie one end of it to the entrance of the cave and follow the rope on his way out of the cave. Theseus placed a nail at the entrance of the cave, tied one end of the yarn to it and began exploring the cave. He did so by leaving a trail of rope behind him and finally found the monster. He caught Minotaur, who extorted Crete, while sleeping and killed him. He left the cave with the help of the rope. He took with him the young people whom he saved from being sacrificed, and Ariadne, and set off. They took a break on the island of Naxos. Some legends have it that Theseus quickly grew tired of Ariadne and left her there, while others tell that god Dionysus saw Ariadne here and stole her from Theseus. Either way, Theseus returned to Athens without Ariadne. However, he had forgotten to hoist a white flag on his ship. When his father saw the black flag, he thought his son, with whom he reunited after long years, was dead and jumped off the rocks into the sea. This sea was later named as Aegeus Pontus, the Aegean Sea, after King Aegeus. Following the death of his father, Theseus became the king of Athens. He was a good king who protected and defended his people. He participated in the Calydonian hunt and the voyage of the Argonauts. He fought against the Amazons. The Amazons attacked Athens to take revenge for Hippolyte, their queen killed by Heracles, and for Antiope kidnapped by Theseus. Even though they besieged the city for a long time, they returned without conquering it.

Theseus had a son named Hippolytus from Antiope, queen of Amazons. After Antiope died, Theseus married Phaedra, the daughter of Minos. However, Phaedra fell in love with Theseus's son Hippolytus. This young man was slandered when he did not return the love of his step-mother. Phaedra told the king that his son attempted to kidnap her. Theseus believed in this calumny and implored the gods that his son be punished. Poseidon startled the horses that drew the chariot of Hippolytus and thus caused his death (Euripides, Hippolytus). When the sad truth became known, Phaedra killed herself. Theseus tried to continue his life in a pathetic way. He had two sons from Phaedra, who were named Acamas and Demophon. Theseus became friends with King Pirithous of the Lapiths. On the wedding of Hippodameia and Pirithous, the invited centaurs overstepped the limit and Theseus killed them. Later Theseus went to Sparta and abducted Helen, who was only twelve years old. Theseus attempted to abduct Persephone, the wife of Hades, together with his friend Pirithous. But Hades caught the two friends and had them sit on the chair of forgetfulness which was tied with snakes.

Heracles salvaged Theseus, but Pirithous was left behind bewildered. When Theseus finally came back to Athens, he saw that things were troublous there. Therefore, he chose to go the island of Skyros and died there due to the betrayal of King Lycomedes. Depictions of Theseus, just like those of Heracles, show him with a thick stick and lion's hide. He differs from Heracles in that Heracles has a more husky body.

Heracles

Alcmene, the daughter of King Electryon of Mycenae, was persuaded to marry the son of his uncle, Amphitryon, who accidentally killed her father. However, she first asked her husband to punish the Taphians who killed her siblings, and her husband left to fulfill her wish. In his absence, Zeus came into the bed of Alcmene, disguised as her husband, and made love to her all day long. Around this time, her husband returned and he made love to his wife as well. Alcmene gave birth to Heracles and Iphicles, with one-day interval, and her husband cherished both of the newborns. In fact, Heracles was from Zeus, and only Iphicles was from Amphitryon, a mortal. Zeus's wife Hera, on the other hand, already knew about this fact and began planning revenge in resentment. One day, while the eight-month old twins were sleeping in their cradles, Hera sent forth two snakes to suffocate the babies. As Iphicles screamed in fear, Heracles killed both of the snakes by throttling them. Heracles was well-educated and was a strong young man when he became eighteen. One day, while watching the herds of his father, he killed the wild and ferocious lion of Cythaeoron, which had been consternating his own people and those of the land of King Thespius. During this fifty-day hunting, King Thespius allowed him to sleep with his fifty daughters. However, every night, Heracles returned home exhausted and was not able to tell that they were all different girls. In the end, he had fifty children from these fifty girls. After this, he fought with and killed King Erginus of Orchomenus, who was extorting the Thebans. As a reward, King Creon of Thebes gave him his daughter Megara, and gave Iphicles his little daughter.

Heracles had one more child from this girl, but Hera cause Heracles to run amuck and kill all of his children. When Heracles came to his senses, he took refuge in Thespius and endeavored to be purified from his crimes. Hera intervened in this as well and informed Heracles through the oracle of Apollo that he should start serving Eurystheus. If he could complete the twelve-year service for redemption from his crimes, he was going to be set free.

Eurystheus was the son of King Sthenelus of Argos. When Zeus impregnated Alcmene, Perseus announced that the first child to be born from his grandchildren was to attain kingship. To prevent Heracles, who

Statue of young Heracles. 2ⁿᵈ century AD. Aphrodisias Museum.

was to be born of Alcmene, from attaining kingship, Hera commissioned her daughter Eileithyia, the midwife goddess, to ensure that the wife of Sthenelus have a premature birth. Thus Eurystheus was born seven months old and became the king of the region of Mycenae, Tiryns and Argolis. A brutal king, Eurystheus was torturing Heracles, who was given to his service, assigning him to the toughest duties. Heracles would be able to repent from his crimes if he could accomplish them. Let us now shortly discuss the twelve challenging duties of Heracles:

The first labor of Heracles was to kill the Nemean lion. The region of Nemea was terrorized by a lion that was born to Typhoon and the Echidna monster. The second labor of Heracles involved his struggle against the dragon named Hydra, who was a snake with nine heads. Hera unleashed this fearsome creature to the swamp of Lerna in the region of Argos. Heracles's duty was to kill this snake. At the end of the battle, Heracles killed the monster by splitting the venomous heads of the snake one by one and smashing his head under a rock. He smeared the venomous bile of the snake onto his arrows. Thus Heracles obtained arrows which slashed incurable wounds.

The third labor of Heracles involved his struggle with the scary boar on Mount Erymanthos in Arcadia. King Eurystheus wanted Heracles to catch the boar alive and bring it to him. During this duty, Heracles was hosted by Pholus the centaur. One day, he got into an argument with the centaur. He killed many centaurs during this argument. Later, Heracles caught the boar with a net after a long pursuit and brought it to the king. The king hid inside a barrel when he saw this scary boar.

His fourth labor was to kill the enchanted deer of Kyrenia, which had golden horns, bronze feet and was protected by Apollo and Artemis. Because this deer was sacred, it was forbidden to kill it. Therefore, Heracles had to chase him for one year. Ultimately he wounded it with his arrows, caught it and brought it to Eurystheus.

Heracle's fifth labor was to kill the eagles around Lake Stymphalia in Arcadia, which had bronze beaks and claws and fed on human meat. Heracles finally accomplished this task too, by scaring these terrifying eagles with the help of the bells given by Athena and shooting them with his arrows.

The sixth labor of Heracles was to clean the stables of Augias. King Augias of Elis had a large number of animals. Therefore, his stables became unusable due to the large piles of manure. Eurystheus assigned this task to Heracles to condescend him. Heracles ensured the cleaning of these stables by changing the courses of the two rivers in this region. In return for this task, the king was going to give Heracles one tenth of his herds. However, he did not keep his promise, and Heracles killed him and his children.

The seventh labor of Heracles was to kill the Cretan bull. King Minos of Crete had promised the god Poseidon to sacrifice a white bull when he attained the throne. But he did not keep his promise. To take revenge, Poseidon infuriated the bull and unleashed it to the wilderness. The bull ate the crops and caused great damage to Crete. Heracles tamed the bull and took it to Greece by holding it from its horns.

His eighth labor was to tame the horses of King Diomedes of Thrace. Heracles fought and killed Diomedes and fed him to his human-eating horses. Thus the horses were tamed. He took the tamed horses to Mycenae.

The ninth labor awaiting Heracles was to steal the magical girdle of the Amazonian queen Hippolyte. Admete, who was the daughter of Eurystheus, asked for the magical girdle given by Ares to the Amazon queen Hippolyte. Heracles killed the queen of the Amazons, who are assumed to have lived on the Black Sea coast, and took her girdle. The tenth labor of Heracles was to bring the herds of Geryoneous. After he accomplished this task too, he plunged into the eleventh one. This duty was to bring the golden apples of the western girls. These magical fruits, which Hera had received as wedding gifts on her wedding to Zeus, were protected by the nymphs and a dragon in the garden of the western girls. Heracles learned from Nereus which path to follow and found the garden of the western girls. In another legend, Heracles rescues Prometheus in Caucasia, who was bound to chains, and learned from him the place of the garden of the western girls. Thus Heracles found the way to the garden of the western girls. He met there Atlas who was carrying the world on his shoulders. Atlas was the only one who could take the golden apples. Heracles took over the duty of Atlas and sent him to take the apples. The giant brought the golden apples but refused to carry the burden of the world again. Heracles deceived him and ran away and offered the apples to Athena.

Heracles's twelfth labor was to rescue the three-headed hound of hell, Cerberus, from the land of the dead. This duty was the hardest among all duties of Heracles. This is because, until that time, nobody was able

Roman sarcophagus illustrating the twelve labors of Heracles.
Konya Archaeology Museum.

to come back from the underworld alive. He went into the underworld
with the help of Hermes and Athena, and met many heroes there. He
returned to the earth finally, taking with him Cerberus the hound. When
King Eurystheus saw this enormous beast, he was frightened out of his
wits. Therefore, Heracles took the dog back to Hades.

These were the main but not the only achievements of Heracles; his
ordeal never came to an end. He returned to Thebes. He gave his first
wife Megara to his friend Ioalaus. He won an archery competition held
by King Eurytus of Oechalia. However, the king did not give his daughter
to Heracles, as he had promised. Heracles ran amuck again and killed
Iphitos, the son of King Eurytus, by throwing him down off the ramparts.
After he came to his senses, he wanted to repent again, but nobody
accepted him. Ultimately, the oracle of Delphi said that he had to be
sold in the market as a slave. Thus, Heracles was sold to the widow
Queen Omphale of Lydia as a slave. This woman treated Heracles
contemptuously. She made him disguised as a woman and sliver. Heracles
was finally redeemed. Later, he took revenge from King Laomedon of
Troy. He married Meleager's sister Deianira. He had a son from her

named Hyllus. Deianira was in love with Achelous, the river god. He had
to wrestle with this river god because of his wife. He was exiled to
Thessaly around this time. One day, he asked Nessus the centaur to pass
his wife Deianira to the other side of the river. He realized that Nessus
was about to kill his wife midway through the river and he shot him with
the arrows that were soaked in the venom of Hydra the snake. Having
been shot by the venomous arrows of Heracles, Nessus wished to take
revenge from Heracles while breathing his last. Before dying, Nessus
gave Deianira a magical potion. He told her to smear this potion on
Heracle's shirt when his love for her diminished, and to have him wear
this. She believed in this lie, accepted the potion thinking it could be
necessary one day, and kept it until the day she would use it. Heracles
joined an archery contest organized by King Eurytus of Oechalia. The
winner was to take the daughter of the king. At the end of the game,
Heracles won. He killed the king for not keeping his promise and took his
daughter Iole as hostage. The word spread that Heracles lost his heart
to this girl. Deianira remembered the magical potion that Nessus had
given her. When Heracles asked his wife for a shirt, Deianira smeared the
potion, which in fact was poison, onto the shirt and gave it to her
husband. The moment he wore the shirt, Heracles began to writhe in

Sarcophagus of Heracles from the 2nd century AD. Antalya Archaeology Museum.

unbearable pain. The shirt stuck to his body, and as he tried to pull it off from his skin, it would come off with his flesh. The poison in the shirt permeated his body at an ever increasing pace, leaving him suffering. Only then did his wife understand that she was deceived, and killed herself. Heracles knew that his end was drawing near. He sent his son Hyllus to Mount Oeta to build a pyre for him there. He gave his friend Philoctetes his bow and arrows and asked him to ignite the woods. Finally, Heracles's sorrows came to an end. Zeus took this suffering son of his to Olympus, reconciled him with Hera, and had him marry Hera's daughter Hebe. Thus he joined the league of immortal gods.

The symbol of heroism, Heracles was gallant in the eyes of the Greeks, who punished the evil and those who did not honor their promises, and overcame the misfortunes experienced by human beings. He was a national hero. He symbolized the invincibility of the human, its power to assault and withstand. His real name was Alcides. This derives from his grandfather Alcaeus. The oracle of Pythia changed this name of his as Heracles, meaning the fame of Hera and hero. This giant human was also accepted as a god. The children of Heracles ruled in the Peloponnese,

thus he was also considered as the ancestor of the Greek peninsula. Therefore, it is possible to find his name in almost every legend or poem. The stories told in the legends became a source of inspiration to sculptors, who revived Heracles in their statues as young, middle-aged and old.

Many writers told the adventures of Heracles. Foremost among them were Ovid and Apollodorus. His fight with snakes during his infancy was written by Theocritus and Pindar. Furthermore, Euripides and Sophocles, who lived in the 5th century BC, wrote many adventures of Heracles in the form of stage play. Many sculptors used these stories in depicting the adventures of Heracles. These were especially illustrated on sarcophagi. Heracles's twelve duties were embossed on sarcophagi, as can be seen in Konya Archaeology Museum and Antalya Museum. There are many statues of Heracles not only in Turkey, but also in major world museums such as the Louvre and British museums. Heracles was depicted as strong and imposing in his statues. He was sometimes shown as leaning on the wand, and sometimes as sitting thoughtfully. The hide of the lion he killed, a thick wand, bow and quiver were his main signs.

Heracles was known as Hercules in Rome, where the hero with identical characteristics was attributed new stories.

MVNIFICENTIA ·SS· D· N· BENEDICTI
PP· XIV· A· D· MDCCLIII·
PIVS· SEXTVS· P· M· REST

Myths, which developed over the centuries by enriching one another, underpin Greek culture. Many of the Greek myths either take place in Anatolia or are related to Anatolia. Some of the myths originated in Anatolia and passed to Greece, while others originated in Greece and developed in Anatolia. There are also legends which first appeared in Phoenicia, Mesopotamia and Egypt, and passed to Anatolia and then to Greece. Therefore, it would be wrong to merely categorize them all as Greek Mythology. These are common legends of the Mediterranean Region. Let us learn about the ones that took place in Anatolia.

Amazons

In ancient times, another favorite and recurrent theme in fine arts was the Amazons, warrior women of Anatolia. They first lived on the foothills of the Caucuses and were later brought to the Black Sea coast by their queen Lysippe. They made Themiscyra their capital, which was situated on the estuary of the River Terme flowing into the Black Sea. Pindar makes it clear that Themiscyra was where Amazons lived. Author Cevat Şakir Kabaağaç, also known as the Fisherman of Halicarnassus, shares the same idea as recorded in his book "Anadolu Efsaneleri" (Legends of Anatolia).

Azra Erhat also maintains that almost all of the legends that originated in Anatolia reflect real incidents and depict real persons, and thus they have an element of truth and a historical attribute to them. As suggested by Erhat, Amazons, also a reality, were extensively used as a theme for many statues, reliefs and vase images. They were depicted as wearing a light-weight garment which came down from their right shoulder to the hips and was tied over the hip with a band. Their arms, legs and feet were naked and they wore a helmet. They were illustrated while fighting on their bareback horses using only a bridle, spreading terror with their double-faced axes, spears and arrows. They used moon-shaped shields symbolizing their mother goddess.

Some scholars claim that the Amazons, the daughters of the god Ares and Harmonia, cut one of their breasts as a young girl, in order to

A Roman-era copy of the Amazon statue by Kresilas.

stretch the bows better, because "mazon" means breast and Amazon must allude to women without breasts. But in contrast to this widely-accepted claim, it is seen in many of the reliefs and sculptures of Amazons that they had two healthy breasts. Another claim on this issue is that "A" in Amazon refers to power and "mazon" means "breast", so Amazon should not be accepted as "without breast", but instead should be understood as referring to female warriors that fight like men. A third claim is that 'a' is a negation prefix, like in Turkish, and "mazo" means "to touch" and thus Amazon meant women who never allowed men to touch them.

Other scholars claimed that "maza" means "moon" in the old Caucasian language, which is because the Amazons worshiped the goddess of the moon, and Cybele, the goddess of Anatolia.

In the fight, other than bows and arrows, Amazons also used double-faced axes which were known as the labrys of the Hittites. This should be additional proof showing that Amazons were Anatolian women. Moreover, many scholars also claim that Amazons were the warrior women of the Hittites.

Although commonly referred to as a legend, the Amazons were real. They governed themselves without having any men to rule them. In order to have children, they would sleep with a man they chose once a year. Among the Amazons, in contrast to other tribes, daughters had more importance. They would give their sons to the father and take care of the daughters themselves.

Many Amazons are mentioned in the affairs of Greek heroes, as in the case of Heracles and Hippolyte, Theseus and Antiope, Achilles and Penthesilea. Heracles was sort of a national hero symbolizing the invincible power of assault and resilience of human against nature. He helped humanity countless times by destroying and eliminating the natural disasters and evils. However, he had a tragic life himself. He was doomed to the anger of Hera from the day he was born. He was given 12 labors by Hera to redeem from his wrongdoings. One of these twelve labors was to bring back the magical golden belt given to the Amazon Queen Hippolyte by Ares. Heracles went to the land of the Amazons together with the gallant Theseus of Athens. The queen

Roman-era copy of the Amazon statue carved by Polycleitus in 430 BC. The Metropolitan Museum of Art in New York.

welcomed Heracles with courtesy and gave him her golden belt as a gift. However, Hera, the enemy of Heracles, disguised as an Amazon and caused a massive disorder, during which the queen was killed by Heracles, while Theseus kidnapped Antiope, the sister of the queen, to Athens. This legend was used as a theme on many sarcophagi and mosaics. In an attempt to rescue their queen, the Amazons attacked Athens led by Orithtyia, the sister of Antiope, yet they were defeated, and Antiope died there.

Greek writers who lived in the 5th century BC such as Socrates and Plato also recorded the attack of the Amazons to Athens as a historical reality. It is told that cities on the Aegean such as Pitane, Myrina, Cyme, and even Ephesus and Smyrna (İzmir) were founded by the Amazons. Moreover, the Alexandrian poet Callimachus wrote that the Amazons built a sculpture in Ephesus in the name of the goddess Artemis and danced around it clashing their shields together, the sound of which could be heard from Sardis. In the 5th century BC, a contest to build an Amazon Statue was held among the contemporary sculptors. This statue was to be placed in the Temple of Artemis in Ephesus, one of the Seven Wonders of the World. According to the accounts of Plinius, the most famous sculptors of the time, Phidias, Polycleitus, Kresilas and Phradmon, competed in the contest. When the sculptures were ready, the sculptors were asked to choose the best. Every sculptor chose his own to be the best, but they all decided that the one carved by Polycleitus was the second best. Consequently, the Amazon statue which they commonly chose to be the second was entitled to be the winner and to be put in the temple.

Roman copies of these Amazon sculptures created by these famous sculptors around 430 BC, appeared in various museums. For example, the Roman copy of the famous Amazon Sculpture created by Phidias is in the Vatican Museum; the Roman Copy of the Amazon Sculpture made by Polycleitus is in the Metropolitan Museum; the Roman marble copy of the Bronze Amazon Sculpture made by Kresilas is in the Copenhagen Museum. Another branch of art that favored Amazons as a theme, in addition to sculpture and frieze, was the art of vase-painting. We can see this clearly from the vases dating to the 5th century BC.

Roman-era copy of the bronze Amazon statue carved by Kresilas in 430 BC. Copenhagen Glyptotek Museum.

Another incident that the Amazons took part in was the Trojan War of around 1200 BC. Amazons went to help Troy with twelve commanders led by their queen Penthesilea. Penthesilea, the queen of Amazons, who became the commander of the army after the death of Hector, confronted Achilles (who could only be shot in his heel and would not be hurt anywhere else and would thus kill whomever he came across). The spear she shot went in vain, however, the arrow shot by Achilles hit the queen on her right breast and knocked her down. At that moment, the helmet of the queen fell on the ground, and Achilles saw that his rival was actually an exceedingly beautiful woman. However, the queen died soon, and Achilles mourned the death of her love, despite having seen her only for a few moments.

The Fisherman of Halicarnassus once said that, none of the legends, which were believed by the Ancient Greeks and attached a national meaning, was as intriguing as that of the Amazons.

In Europa, the Amazons continued to be the center of attraction during the Renaissance. For instance, Francisco de Orellana gave the name Amazon to the river which she reached in America in 1542, because of the native women living there. Homer's Iliad is known as the oldest source that mentions the Amazons, in which Amazons are referred to as "manlike women". Later, Strabo talks about their traditions and cities under Chapter IV of his "Geographica".

They seemingly disappeared around 700 BC. It is assumed that they migrated from Anatolia back to Caucasia together with the warriors coming form that region. The graves of female warriors in Ukraine support this claim.

Wars between the Greeks and the Amazons (Amazonomachy) were a very popular theme among the artists and sculptors in the 5th century BC. It is seen that this theme was also used on metope-reliefs of the Treasury House of Athens in Delphi. The Temple of Apollo in Eretria, which dates to around 510 BC, also uses the kidnapping of Antiope as a theme. Furthermore, the Temple of Zeus at Olympia and the Temple of Hera at Selinas, as well as other parts of Anatolia, also have depictions of this intriguing war.

The friezes on the Lycian grave monument in Gölbaşı and the Tempe of Artemis at Magnesia near Söke illustrate the wars of Amazon. On these friezes, which reach 174 m. in length, 347 people were depicted.

Part of the friezes, measuring 134m in length, is located in the İstanbul Archaeology Museum today, while the other parts are in the Berlin Museum and the Louvre Museum in Paris.

Another frieze showing the Amazons is the monumental tomb that was made for Satrap Maussollos of Caria in 350 BC. The Amazon friezes which decorate the monument were crafted by the famous sculptors of that time, Leochares, Bryaxis, Scopas and Timotheus.

This monumental tomb, one the Seven Wonders of the World, was destroyed by an earthquake in the 15th century. The stones of it were used by the Knights of Rhodes for castle building, while the friezes were used to decorate the walls.

The way these friezes and sculptures, which are kept in British Museum today, were taken to England is another story. In 1846, Lord Stratford Canning was the English ambassador to İstanbul and he wanted the friezes in Bodrum. After his endeavors, the Sultan Abdulmecid gave him the friezes as a gift.

Telephus

In Pausanias's accounts, Aleus the king of Tegea in Arcadia learned from a seer in Delphi that the children of his daughter Auge were going to kill their uncles. To prevent this prophecy, he made his daughter a nun at the Temple of Athena. Yet, the prophecy was fulfilled. During his visit to the region, Heracles fell in love with this girl and impregnated her. When king Aleus found this out, he gave his daughter to the sailor Nauplius, who was supposed to drown her. On the way, her labor pains began, so the sailor took her to Mount Parthenion. There, she gave birth to a boy. The sailor left the child alone on the mountain, spared the life of Auge but took her to Mysia and sold her there. The baby was suckled by a hind on the mountain and then raised by shepherds. He was named Telephus, which means deer.

When Telephus reached adolescence, he killed two people involuntarily. These were his uncles. He asked the wise men how he could be cleansed from this sin, and they told him to go to Mysia and enter into the service of King Teuthras. Telephus came to Mysia, found the king and the king adopted him.

The king promised to give Auge (in fact Telephus's mother) to him if he helped him against his enemy Idas. When Telephus helped the king, the king gave the hand of the girl to him. However, this horrible incident was prevented by the intervention of the gods, and Auge married King Teuthras. After a while, Teuthras died and Telephus became the king of Mysia. Around this time, the Achaeans initiated an expedition to Troy. When they mistakenly disembarked on the shores of Mysia, instead of Troy, they had to fight King Telephus. Although Telephus fought and killed many Achaeans, he was injured by Achilles. The Achaeans turned back to their land but the wound of Telephus would not heal. The seers told him that his wound would only be healed by the rust of the weapon of the person who injured him, so he went to Greece. The Achaean troops gathered for a new expedition at the Port of Aulis. Telephus approached Achilles there, disguised as a beggar. His identity, however, was soon revealed and he had to make a deal with Achilles; he was going to show them the way to Troy in return for the rust of his spear. Achilles applied the rust of the spear to his wound, and it began to heal quickly.

It was now time for him to show the way to Troy. He kept his promise and guided the Achaeans towards Troy, but did not join the war on the side of the Trojans even though he was married to the sister of Priam. However, his son Eurypylus came to help Priam with a small Mysian troop. When Telephus returned, he left the old capital city Teuthrania and founded Pergamum. He was therefore accepted by the people of Pergamum as their founding king. When the Temple of Zeus was being built around 170 BC, King Eumenes II commemorated their founder by commissioning 30 reliefs of Telephus to be built in the altar. In the Hellenistic Period, Pergamum continued to be a free and powerful kingdom until 133 BC, but when Attalus III died and bequeathed his lands to Rome, Pergamum came under the rule of Rome.

Musical Competition of Apollo and Marsyas

This legend, which we learn from the writer Ovid, takes place on the foothills of Mount Tmolus in the Aegean. Here, the subject is the musical competition between Apollo and Marsyas under the arbitration of the mountain god Tmolus.

The flute was invented by the goddess Athena. While playing the flute, she saw her reflection on the water with puffy cheeks and did not like her appearance. She became angry and threw the flute away, saying that

Statue of Dionysus and Satyr dating to 160-180 BC. Burdur Museum.

whoever found the flute and blew into it would be punished greatly and cursed by her. The victim of this curse became Marsyas, who played the flute every day in joy. He mastered this skill and began to boast that he could play the flute better than Apollo's lyre. As he kept bragging about it everywhere, Apollo heard of him. As a result, a musical competition was held between the two. The condition was that the winner of the competition was going to punish the other in whatever way he wanted. The mountain god Tmolus and the King Midas of Phrygia judged the competition. Marsyas who played his flute, and when it was his turn, Apollo played his lyre ardently. In the end, Tmolus chose Apollo and Midas chose Marsyas to be the winner. Then, Apollo showed another trick with his lyre by playing it in reverse and challenged Marsyas. Marsyas was not able to blow into his flute in reverse, so Apollo won the competition and deserved to punish Marsyas. Apollo had Marsyas hung on a tree and had him skinned alive. This was to prevent any mortal from attempting to compete with immortals in the future. However, later, Apollo regretted his decision and broke his lyre and transformed Marsyas into a river. This incident was a popular theme for sculptors in ancient times. Marsyas is shown hanging on a tree, while a slave sharpens his knife. The pain on the face of Marsyas is well reflected in such works of artists. The sculptures of Marsyas depicting him with thick

Statue of Marsias.
İstanbul Archaeology
Museums.

beard and in pain, can be seen in museums such as the İstanbul Archaeology Museum, Antalya Museum and Louvre Museum.

Apollo also punished Midas the king of Phrygia as he said that he liked the flute of Marsyas. He said that ears which could not appreciate good music were donkey's ears and turned the ears of Midas into donkey's ears. Poor Midas tried to hide his ears with a Phrygian hat. After a while, his hair grew long and he had had to call for his hairdresser to cut his hair. When he took off his hat, which he never did before, his donkey's ears became apparent and the hairdresser saw them. Midas warned him to keep it a secret. However, the hairdresser could not resist but shouted the secret into a hole, *"Did you know that King Midas had donkey's ears?"* Later, the reeds growing near the hole echoed his voice every time the wind blew. Midas is famous for this story, but in fact, Midas was the King of Phrygia who participated

in many wars. In the late Assyrian sources, he is referred to as "Mita" who signed agreements with the Assyrian people. In 695 BC, Midas committed suicide by drinking the blood of a bull because he was not able to stop the Cimmerian raids from the north. Today, his tomb is in Gordion near Polatlı. Found on top of his tomb were numerous grave chambers containing the belongings of Midas.

Dionysus and Midas

One day, Midas's men brought before him a satyr follower of Dionysus, who had oozed under a tree. Midas hosted him in his palace for 10 days and took him back to the god Dionysus. Dionysus became exceedingly content by this gesture and granted Midas a wish. Midas wished that everything he touched became gold; however, Dionysus warned him that his wish my cause him troubles. Midas insisted and his wish was fulfilled, after which he took leave of Dionysus. He realized that the crops he touched on his way turned into gold. This amused Midas so much that he ordered a sumptuous feast be prepared when he came back to his palace. However, the bread he touched and the wine glass he grabbed turned into gold as well. Midas repented and asked Dionysus for forgiveness. Dionysus saved him from this misery.

Niobe

Another legend that originated in Anatolia and developed in Greece was that of Niobe. Niobe, the daughter of King Tantalus of Lydia, grew up with Leto on the plain of Manisa. When she reached the age of marriage, her father made her marry the Theban king Amphion. Six daughters and six sons were born from this marriage. Niobe, who was always proud of her children, would boast that her childhood friend Leto had only two children while she had a dozen. Her boasting outraged Leto, the mother of two gods. Leto asked her children to kill the children of Niobe. They did what their mother asked them to do and killed the children of Niobe by shooting them with their arrows.

Niobe mourned over the dead bodies of her children for days and eventually she turned into a rock. Today on Mount Manisa, there is a "Weeping Stone," where the tip of stone is accepted to be Niobe's head and the spring water coming from this stone is accepted to be her tears.

Bellerophontes

Bellerophontes was the child of Glaucus, who was the son of Sisyphus. He came from the lineage of Poseidon. For that reason, he had deific features. He was keen on horses like his father. One day, he saw the flying horse Pegasus in the sky and fell in love with it. After that day, he thought of nothing but to capture it. He pursued it for days, weeks and months, but he could not capture it. One day, while sleeping under an olive tree, he had a dream in which the goddess Athena gave him a bridle and told him that he could catch Pegasus only with that bridle. When Bellerophontes woke up, he found a golden bridle next to him. Before long, he caught Pegasus with this bridle and owned him.

One day, Bellerophontes killed one of his relatives by mistake. He was therefore expelled from his country and took shelter in the palace of King Proteus of Tryns in the Argos region. After a short while, Anteia, the wife of the king, fell in love with this young man and wanted to sleep with him. However, Bellerophontes chose not to betray the king, and refused the request of the queen because he was the guest of the King. The fact that she could not seduce him offended the womanly pride of the queen. Therefore, she slandered the young man who refused to sleep with him. She told her husband that Bellerophontes tried to sleep with her forcefully. The woman, who insanely sought revenge and wanted him to be killed. However, the king did not want to kill him and wanted somebody else to do this for him. He sent him to his father-in-law Iobates, the King of Lycia in Anatolia, while also dispatching a letter explaining the situation. The king welcomed the guest by the Xanthos River and he sacrificed nine oxen for nine consecutive days in the name of the guest. On the tenth day, he received the letter from his son-in-law. The letter requested the death of Bellerophontes in code.

King Iobates believed that this young visitor was holy and he could not dare to kill him. After entertaining him as a guest in his palace for a while, he decided to have the fiery Chimera kill him. Chimera was a strange monster; the front part of her body was a lion; the middle part of it was a goat and the back part of it was a snake. She scattered flames from her mouth. Bellerophontes killed her with the arrows and spears he shot from above, flying on his winged-horse Pegasus. The burning of gas in the Ancient City of Olympus in Lycia is believed to be the flames coming from the mouth of Chimera.

Following this, King Iobates gave other tasks to Bellerophontes, but he managed to survive all of them. He even survived the trap set by the bravest men of the king, on his way back. After all this, the king was convinced that he was a descendent of gods. He first showed the letter to him, and later gave the hand of his daughter in marriage to him as a sign of peace. Bellerophontes had three children named Isandrus, Hippolochus and Laodamia from this marriage. When these children grew up, Zeus slept with Laodamia, the daughter of Bellerophontes. From this relationship, the famous King Sarpedon of Lycia, who came to help Troy, was born.

Eros and Psyche

Psyche, another female character from an Anatolian legend, means life or soul. The Latin writer Apuleius tells this story in his "Metamorphoses". This legend, which is originally from Miletus, stems from the envy of Aphrodite.

Eros was defined as the symbol of love and passion, and he made people fall in love with each other with his arrow. Since the early texts of ancient times, he is depicted as the power ensuring love and reproduction. Hesiod recites him right after Chaos because he was believed to be present during the day the world was created. Eros, who was believed to be the son of Aphrodite and Hermes, was called 'Amor-Amore' in Rome and was a popular theme among poets and artists. Since Eros denoted love and Psyche denoted soul, they were inseparable from each other. However their union was achieved after so many hardships. Aphrodite who envied the beauty of Psyche told her son Eros to make this girl fall in love with a dragon. Eros found the girl, directed his arrow at her but he fell in love with Psyche. He took her to a palace and visited her only at nights. His lover could not see him but could feel his body. He told her not to ever try to see him. But she wondered whether the man next to her could actually be a dragon and not a good-looking young man.

When one day she went to visit her family, they asked her what her husband looked like and she answered that she had never seen him.

Statue of Hermaphrodite. 3rd century BC. İstanbul Archeology Museums.

Her sisters convinced her that she was married to a dragon and that she should leave him. They told her that she could see him with a candle while he was asleep. When Eros slept, she did what she was told to do and saw a very handsome young man beside her. She became excited from what she saw; her hands began to shake and a candle drop fell on Eros' shoulder. Eros woke up and flew away from her, never to come back. After a while, neither of them could forget each other, and they began to be consumed by their love. Finally, Aphrodite felt sorry for them and accepted to allow them to be together on certain conditions, which were hard to accomplish. Yet the nymphs and spirits helped Psyche and she accomplished all the tasks. Eventually, Eros took the immortality drink named "ambrosia" from Zeus and had her drink it, thus the human soul became immortal. Eros told her that they would live together and teach people to love each other. Youth and happiness were born from this couple.

Hermaphroditus and Salmacis

The legend of Hermaphroditus takes place on Salmacis Lake situated opposite of the Bodrum Castle. A naiad nymph called Salmacis lived in this small and translucent lake. This nymph would collect flowers and enjoy swimming in the lake, which was surrounded by greenery. She would comb her wet hair with a wooden comb and watch herself in the lake water.

According to the Latin poet Ovid, one day, the beauty goddess Aphrodite and the messenger god Hermes slept together and had a baby. The baby was named "Hermaphroditus", the combination of the names of the mother and the father. In order to hide her sins, Aphrodite abandoned her child to the nymphs of Mount Ida after the birth. When Hermaphroditus reached the age of fifteen, he wanted to see different countries and arrived in Caria. Eventually he reached the lake near Halicarnassus. The nymph Salmacis saw this godlike young man and approached him by saying that he must be a god, and if he was a god, he must be Eros, the god of love, and that her mother must be proud of him, and that his wife would be very lucky, and that all she wanted from him was a short fling.

Hermaphroditus was a shy young man; he did not know what to do. He only told the nymph to go away and pushed her. Salmacis was disappointed and hid behind a bush.

Later, Hermaphroditus thought he was alone and became naked, and entered into the lake. Salmacis could not resist and she also entered into lake. She embraced the young man who looked like a sculpture in pure water. She told him that there was no way he could escape her now and began kissing him like crazy. While the young man was trying to escape, she embraced him more tightly and begged the gods not to separate them from each other. The gods accepted her prayer and granted her wish. Now there was only one body in the lake. This was neither a man nor a woman. After that incident, people having both sex organs came to be called hermaphrodites.

Hermaphroditus begged the gods that whoever entered that lake should come out as half female and half male, and the gods accepted his wish too. Strabon states that this lake had such an effect even during his time.

Waters coming out of the rocks in the Salmacis Bay used to form little ponds until very recently. In fact, the ancient writers tell us that the temples of both Hermes and Aphrodite were located on the rocky area known as Kaplan Kayası, which rises just above the coast.

Arachne

In the legend which takes place in Colophon in the Aegean, Arachne, the beautiful daughter of Idmon, would embroider, knit and weave carpets. No one could embroider, or weave carpets better than her. Nymphs watched this girl, who was always proud of and boastful about her abilities, with admiration. When, one day, a nymph asked her if she learned these great abilities from Athena, she answered that she learned them by herself and she was better than her. She even claimed that she could compete with Athena. When Athena, who was famous for her weaving abilities, heard this, she became very angry and went to Colophon disguised as an old woman. She gave her advice, told her to be modest and avoid challenging the goddesses. However, she was not able make herself heard to the prideful Arachne. Athena then transformed into a goddess again and told her that she was ready to compete. The competition started. Athena embroidered the Olympian gods on her frame and Arachne embroidered the love affairs of Zeus on hers. When the competition was over, even Athena was surprised at the ability of the girl, but deep inside she was resentful that Arachne was superior to her. Therefore, she tore apart the embroidery of Arachne. Arachne, who could not bear the insult, hanged herself. However, Athena turned her into a spider in order to make her weave forever at the dusty corners of the walls and receive no benefit out of it.

The Legend of Hero and Leander

Being one of the most popular legends of ancient times, this legend takes place in the Dardanelles Strait. There was a city called Abydos on the Anatolian side of the Dardanelles Strait (ancient name Hellespontos) and another city called Sestos on the Europaan side of it. In Abydos lived a prince named Leander and in Sestos lived a beautiful nun of Aphrodite called Hero.

When the winter was over and the spring came, rituals were held at the temple for the dead lover of Aphrodite called Adonis. The temple was full of people coming from various places. Leander also participated in this ritual. Leander, who had just turned 18, was wearing a wreath of leaves. He arrived at the temple holding doves in his hand. When he came closer to the shrine to present the doves, he met the nun Hero who was in charge of the doves at the temple. Leander could not take his eyes off Hero, who wore decorative wreaths made of red roses. Hero reciprocated his feelings.

Leander could not stand staying in Abydos away from Hero and visited her often. One day, he saw a torch on the tower of the temple. He could not wait anymore and jumped into the cold waters and began to swim towards the torch. Even the cold waters of the sea were not able to extinguish the burning flame in his heart. He reached the shore impatiently, and climbed the stairs of the tower. The door of the tower was open. Hero waited there for him. Afterwards, Hero lit her torch every night and Leander swam toward the light from across the shore. The love of these two young people increased every day. However, Hero was a nun and was forbidden from marriage.

The summer ended and it began to be cool. On a night like this, Leander jumped into water again and began swimming against the waves, but a strong wind extinguished the torch in Hero's hand. There was no moon light either. Leander kept swimming, not knowing where he was going, eventually losing his way and strength. His dead body only reached the shore. Hero lit the torch again and ran to the beach.

Suddenly she saw the dead body of her lover and she threw herself into the sea, wanting to meet him after death. The waves brought her dead body next to her lover's. Hence, these two lovers met in the other world.

Endymion and Selene

Today the place where Bafa Lake is situated used to be the Latmos Bay. Located behind this bay was an ancient city called Heraclea. And behind this city rose the mountains which used to be called Latmos and are now known as the Beşparmak Mountains. The bay was seen with all its beauty from the Latmos Mountains. For this reason, the bay was known as 'the mirror of the moon goddess'. The legend of Endymion was born in this place.

Endymion was a handsome shepherd living in the Latmos Mountains. He put his goats out to the field happily and he played his pipe, while the goats jumped from rock to rock and grazed on delicious thyme plants. When the night fell, he would fall asleep on the green grass watching the starry sky, or on cool nights, he would sleep in a nearby cave where nobody could see him. Only the goddess of the moon, Selene, saw him and fell in love with him while watching him with admiration. Every night, she embraced him with her silver light. Selene would stay with her lover sometimes for a long period of time, and sometimes for a short period of time. She never came on dark nights. But the waiting was not long; when the moon appeared in the sky again, Selene and Endymion would meet and make love to their heart's content. The god of the gods saw this love and admired them, so he decided to give a present to the shepherd of the Latmos Mountains. One day, Zeus granted Endymion a wish, and the poor shepherd asked for an eternal sleep from the god. His wish was immediately granted and Endymion fell into an eternal sleep. He slept for days, months and years, but his face retaining its youth and beauty. Today, there are traces of a temple belonging to Endymion in Heraclea near Bafa Lake.

Although various writers associate this beautiful love story with other places, Theocritus, the writer of the story, records that the legend took place on the Latmos Mountains.

THE FOUNDING OF TROY (TROIA) AND THE BIRTH OF PARIS

Iasion and Dardanus, who were born from the union of Zeus and Electra, the daughter of Atlas, grew up on the island of Samothrace (Semendirek in Turkish). When his brother died and the island was submerged by the sea, Dardanus sailed on a raft across to the Anatolian coasts. The king who lived here, Teucer, welcomed this disaster victim, hosted him at his house and gave the hand of his daughter Batea to this young man in marriage and thus making him his son-in-law. When the king died after a while, Dardanus succeeded him on the throne and established the city of Dardanus which was located near today's Çanakkale. Following the death of Dardanus, Erichthonius became the king, and following his death, Tros became the king.

Tros married Callirhoe, the daughter of the River God Scamander. He had three sons in this marriage who were named Ilus, Assaracus and Ganymede. Of these children, Ganymede was the most beautiful of the mortals. Zeus admired him so much and wanted him to live in Olympus among the gods, with all his beauty, so he snatched him to Olympus to serve wine. He gifted King Tros immortal horses in return for this handsome young man. With the death of King Tros, Ilus took the throne in Troy. Ilus participated in a race in the region and he was victorious. He was rewarded with fifty slaves and a black-spotted cow. Seers told Ilus to follow the path of this cow and found a city where it stopped. On the advice of the seers, Ilus came to his land and waited for the cow to stop somewhere. The cow finally stopped on a hilltop, which was upon the the hill of Ate. Ate was the goddess of delusion, who was born of the goddess of strife Eris. Outraged at Ate, Zeus threw her on to the earth, and she landed on the Hill of Ate. This was the hill where the cow stopped. Ilus founded a city here and named it after himself. This city, which was originally known as Ilion and later renamed as Troy, would suffer endless troubles due to the Goddess of Heedlessness.

After founding the city, Ilus asked for an omen from god Zeus on whether his city would be fortunate or not. Zeus answered his wish by descending Palladium from the sky. Palladium was the statue of Athena which had magical attributes. Even though Ilus built a Temple of Athena on the spot where the statue fell, the ill fortune surrounding Troy never ended. After Ilus's death, his son Laomedon assumed the throne in Troy. As Laomedon became king in Troy, some incidents were taking place in Olympus. Apollo, Poseidon and the other gods became angry at Zeus and wanted to set a trap for him and hang him in the sky by shackling him. The god of gods, Zeus, found out about this and punished those gods who plotted this scheme. He took the deific powers from Apollo and Poseidon and instructed them to serve King Laomedon of Troy for one year. Laomedon asked Apollo to herd his cattle, and Poseidon to build splendid city walls in his city which had no walls yet. He told them that he would pay them in return for their services. Thus, the gods agreed and began to work; in one year, the city walls were built and the gods completed their punishment. They asked the king for their payment, but the king failed to keep his promise and did not pay them. The gods obtained their powers again and they wanted to punish the king for not keeping his promise. Apollo sent a plague epidemic, and Poseidon sent a sea monster to the city. King Laomedon was regretful. He was even more devastated when he was told that he had to sacrifice his daughter Hesione to do away with the sea monster. Since there was no choice, he unwillingly accepted his daughter being hanged to the rocks by the sea to be sacrificed to the monster. At that moment, Heracles was on his way back from completing his twelfth labor given by Hera; the snatching of the girdle of the Amazonian queen. He happened to pass by Troy and saw what was happening; he said he could kill the monster but in return, he asked from King Laomedon for the immortal horses given to his grandfather by Zeus. The King promised him that he would give him the horses if he saved his daughter. Heracles saved Hesione by slaying the monster. However, Laomedon forgot about his promise when he saw his daughter was alive and did not want to part from his horses. Thus, Heracles left the city by swearing that he was going to attack it. After a while, he came with his companions and attacked the city. During this attack, he took the daughter and son of the king as hostage. He gave Hesione to his friend Telamon. However, Hesione had a condition. She asked for his brother to be released. Heracles accepted her condition and released the little prince. The prince returned to Troy and became king with the name of Priam. He married Hecuba and nineteen children were born from this marriage including Hector and Cassandra. The first child of Hecuba was Hector. Her second-born son was Paris. Later, Hecuba had four daughters. Following these daughters, who were named Creusa,

Laodice, Polyxena and Cassandra, she gave birth to Deiphobus, Antiphus, Hipponous, Polydorus and her youngest; Troilus.

Hecuba was pregnant with her next child after Hector. One night, he woke from frightening nightmares, in which flames were coming out of her womb and were burning the city. When she asked the seers to interpret this dream, she learned that this child to be born would bring destruction to Troy. The anxious mother and father did not know what to do, so they decided that the child to be born should be sent away so that the holy Troy would not be destroyed.

The child was born after a while, and they gave him to a servant to kill him on Mount Ida. The servant did not have the heart to kill the child, so he left him in a cave to be devoured by wild animals. The inhabitant of the cave was a bear, who nursed and helped the baby survive.

One day, while grazing his herds, a shepherd named Agelaus saw the child and took him home to be raised together with his own children. When Paris grew up, he stood out among the shepherds with his beauty and expediency. He was named "Alexander" meaning "protector" for grazing his herds well. Having been raised in the clean air of Mount Ida, Paris grew into a handsome young man and married a nymph named Oenone.

Paris's Judgment

As Paris continued to live on Mount Ida, some incidents were occurring in Olympus. Nereus, who was the old man of the sea, had fifty daughters. Of these girls, Thetis was eminently beautiful. Zeus and Poseidon lost their heart to this girl, but seers warned that the child to be born of Thetis would exceed his father in power. Therefore, they decided to give her hand to a mortal. They chose Peleus as her husband. Peleus had experienced many events; his wife was dead. Although Thetis did not want to marry such a man chosen by the gods, she unwillingly accepted this. The wedding was to take place in Olympus at the dining table of the gods. Even though all the gods and goddesses were invited to the wedding, the goddess of strife, Eris, was forgotten. She was compelled to take revenge for this by stirring a fight. She pondered and decided to write on a golden apple, "to the most beautiful one", and threw it among the goddesses. She accomplished what she wanted.

Vase illustration of the first beauty contest on Mount Ida, dating to the 4th century BC.

Hera, Athena and Aphrodite all wished to have the apple for themselves claiming that they were the most beautiful one. Since there was no way for them to reconcile, they consulted Zeus. Zeus was cunning enough not to be involved in such a matter, so he appointed Paris, the shepherd on Mount Ida, to make the decision. He commissioned Hermes, the messenger god, to tell the goddesses to go to Mount Ida, where Paris would make a judgement. Whomever he gave the golden apple would be chosen as the most beautiful goddess.

This incident which changed Paris's life began with this judgement. Without delay, the three goddesses went to Mount Ida as accompanied by Hermes. Hermes told Paris of the order of Zeus and gave the golden apple to him. Paris looked at the three goddesses, but could not decide whom to choose. Seeing the hesitation of Paris, Hera went to his ear and said that if he were to choose her as the most beautiful, she would give him the kingdom of Asia, and Athena offered him wisdom, and Aphrodite offered him the love of the most beautiful woman on the earth. Given these tempting offers, Paris extended the apple to Aphrodite, whether or not due to his age. The most beautiful goddess was Aphrodite and all the gods accepted this judgement. However, Hera and Athena harbored an endless grudge against Paris and his city due to his decision.

Shortly after, there was a contest in Troy to choose the best raised bull. Paris took his bull and came to Troy. He participated in the contest and won. He received his prize from the hands of King Priam. Meanwhile, his jealous siblings attempted to kill him, and Paris took shelter in the altar of Zeus. His sister Cassandra understood who he was. Once, Apollo fell in love with Cassandra and gave her the power of seeing the future. However, because his love was not reciprocated, he cursed her; she could still see into the future but nobody would believe her. Thanks to her ability to see, Cassandra knew that Paris was the child left on Mount Ida years ago and said that he had to be killed, otherwise, he would bring destruction to the city, but nobody believed her. On the other hand, when they saw their long-lost child standing before them as a handsome young man, the aged King Priam and Hecuba embraced him with love, let alone killing him. Thus, the shepherd of Mount Ida settled in the palace of Priam as the prince of Troy. While leading a comfortable life in the palace with his siblings, his mind was still occupied with Helen, the most beautiful woman of the world whom Aphrodite promised him.

Helen

Who was the most beautiful woman of the world that Aphrodite offered to Paris? It was Helen, the wife of the Spartan King Menelaus.

Created by Homer in his legends, Helen, with her extraordinary beauty, was the most famous of the legendary persons and has been the subject of endless discussions.

Helen was the daughter of Leda and Zeus, the chief god. When the chief god saw Leda, the wife of the Aetolian King Tyndareus, while bathing in a lake, he lost his heart to her and approached her disguised as a swan. Several accounts are given of this myth, in which this union brings forth two sets of twin babies; identical twins Helen and Polydeuces, and Clytemnestra and Castor. Helen, the subject of countless tales and stories, became outstandingly beautiful with each passing day.

One day, while making an offering to Artemis, she was abducted by Theseus, a brave Athenian. However, her brothers rescued Helen. Helen's father Tyndareus, who was a mortal, feared that his daughter would get into trouble due to her beauty and wanted to give the hand of his daughter as soon as possible. Her suitors were many; one rumor has it that she had 29, another has it that she had 99 suitors. Even though many sons of kings and many brave men in Greece were asking for the hand of Helen, only Achilles was not among them because he was not of marriageable age.

Perplexed by the number of suitors, the father was comforted with the advice of Odysseus. Accordingly, Helen was to choose her husband herself, and the other suitors would swear to look after to protect the chosen husband.

So it happened; Agamemnon took the hand of Helen's sister Clytemnestra, and Helen chose Menelaus as her husband. Agamemnon became king of Mycenae, while Menelaus took the throne in Sparta. Menelaus and Helen lived happily for nine consecutive years, until Paris, the youngest son of the Trojan King Priam, came to Sparta and enamored Helen with the help of Aphrodite.

While Menelaus was in Crete for the funeral of his grandfather, the two lovers took the Spartan treasury with them and ran away to Troy.

EXPEDITION TO TROY

Having found out that his wife ran away to Troy with the Trojan prince Paris, Menelaus asked his older brother Agamemnon, the king of Mycenae, to launch an expedition to Troy to bring back Helen. Agamemnon was already considering capturing Troy because it had the control of the straits and thus prevented trade in the Black Sea. News was sent everywhere in Greece. To honor the oath they had taken, all the previous suitors of Helen joined in the call. Odysseus was not among them. This is because the seers had told him that, if he were to join this war, he would come back home poor and lonely, only after twenty years. Therefore, he avoided the war acting as if he was mentally insane. He sowed salt in his field guiding a plow hitched with a donkey and an ox. When Palamedes came to recruit him, he wanted to test if he was really crazy or not. He grabbed the newborn child of Odysseus, Telemachus, from the arms of its mother and placed it in front of the plow. Odysseus stopped the animals, and it was revealed that he was not crazy. Thus, he arrived at the Port of Aulis together with the crowd gathered for the war. Then Achilles disappeared. The oracles reported that Troy could not be taken without him, so Odysseus went to search for him. However, Achilles's mother launched plots because he knew that he would not come back if he went to war. She sent Achilles to the Skyros Island across from Greece. Achilles was hosted in the palace of King Lycomedes disguised as a girl, and hid among the daughters of the king. One rumor has it that he slept with one of his daughters there, and Neoptelemus was born from this union. Odysseus, who was charged to bring him back, thought of a trick. He approached the girls disguised as a wandering vendor and opened up his bundle of precious fabrics and embroidery. In fact, there were valuable weapons underneath. Achilles saw them and could not help but became interested in them. Thus he was identified. Achilles and Odysseus came to the Port of Aulis, where the Achaean army gathered. When everybody was there, the ships set sail and the expedition to Troy began. However, instead of Troy, the fleet landed on the shores of Mysia, which was further to the south. There, they met Telephus, the founding king of Pergamum. Telephus, who was the son of Heracles and Auge, fought gallantly against the Achaeans and killed a few noteworthy persons, but Achilles wounded him on the thigh. The Achaeans soon realized that they embarked on a wrong place and returned. However, the storm had totally destroyed the fleet. Therefore, they had to return to their home land separately.

Roman-era mosaic depicting the participation of Achilles in the Trojan War. It was found in Zeugma.

IRACE

BYZANTION

BITHYNIA

Perkote

risbe

Kyzikos

Sangarius River
(Sakarya)

S

Antandros

MYSIA

PHRYGIA

Pergamon

AEOLIS

Hermos River (Gediz)

LYDIA

Smyrna

Sardes

Philedelphia

nai

IONIA

Ephesos

Nysa

A

OS

Priene

Maeander River (B.Menderes)

raion

Miletos

Dydima

CARIA

PISIDIA

Halicarnassos

KOS

LYCIA

Knidos

RHODES

Kameiros

Xanthos

Lindes

SEA

THE SECOND EXPEDITION TO TROY

Eight years had passed after the failure of the first expedition to Troy. Achaeans had gathered at the Port of Aulis, which was a deep cove between the Continental Greece and the Euboea (Eğriboz) Peninsula, in the Boeotia Region. Around this time, King Telephus of Mysia came to the Port of Aulis, whom Achilles had wounded on the shores of Anatolia during the first disembarkment. Telephus accepted to show them the way to Troy in return for his wounds being healed. As his wounds healed, the ships to join the expedition began arriving one by one, being docked side by side at the Port of Aulis.

Located in Southern Greece between the Gulf of Argos and the Gulf of Corinth, the Kingdom of Mycenae was the most powerful kingdom of Greece, and the other kingdoms were at its disposal. Mycenaean King Agamemnon was joining this expedition as commander-in-chief. Seemingly preparing for the expedition for his brother Menelaus's cause, Agamemnon was in fact concerned about subduing Troy, which controlled the way to the Black Sea, to be able to engage in trade on the Black Sea easily. Therefore, he prepared to set sail with 100 ships, which was the most crowded of the troops. Menelaus, whose wife ran away to Troy, was the king of Sparta located in Southern Greece. He was joining this expedition with 60 ships for his own cause. Other kingdoms participated with varying numbers of ships and soldiers depending on their strength. For instance, in addition to the Boeotians, who lived near the Port of Aulis and provided 50 ships having 120 soldiers each, the inhabitants of Aspledon provided 30 ships, and the Lilaeans, who lived on the Cephissus River, provided 40 ships for the expedition.

The Locrians, who lived on the Boagrius River, provided 40 ships under the commandment of Aias, the son of Oileus. The Abantes from Euboea, who lived in Cerinthus, came with 40 ships to join the expedition. Also joining this war were the Athenians with 50 ships under the commandment of Menestheus; Aias of Salamis with 12 ships; inhabitants of Aegae, which was located on the edge of a deep gulf, with 80 ships under the commandment of Diomedes. Forces also came to join from Pylus, led by the aged Nestor, together with 90 ships. The Arcadians, who lived on the

Iphigenia being taken by her father Agamemnon and her mother Clytemnestra to be sacrificed. Roman Period. Antakya Museum.

slopes of Mount Cyllene, came under the leadership of Agapenor. They did not have any ships because they lived in a land-locked country, so Agamemnon provided them with 60 ships to ensure that they joined the expedition. Later, the inhabitants of Elis came with 40 ships under the leadership of four commanders. King Odysseus of the island of Ithaca in the Ionian Sea, who was the most cunning and intelligent of the Achaeans, came with 12 ships. Aetolians, who lived in Chalkis, in the rocky Calydon by the sea, came with 40 ships. Idomeneus led the forces coming from Crete. There were 80 ships at his disposal. Rhodians came with 9 ships, Nireus of Syme came with 3 ships, and those coming from Kos and Kalydna Islands took their places with 30 ships.

The commander of the people known as the Myrmidons living in Argos was Achilles. He prepared 50 ships for this expedition, which he involuntarily joined. The Phylaceans took their place near his ships with 40 ships. The inhabitants of Olizon joined with 20 ships under the commandment of Philoctetes, who had the arrows of Heracles. Others came from many different places and a total of hundred thousand people and thousand ships gathered at the Port of Aulis to launch the expedition. Homer refers to all of these forces as the Achaeans and Danaus. The ships ready to set sail were waiting for the order of Agamemnon, commander-in-chief. Finally, he gave the order to depart. But, there was not enough wind to fill the sails of the ships. Everybody asked one another why the wind did not blow. When the seers were asked, Calchas the seer told that Agamemnon hunted the holy deer of Artemis once and Artemis thus hindered the wind. Calchas was also the one who told the way out. If the Agamemnon sacrificed his daughter Iphigenia to Artemis, the wind would start blowing again.

Agamemnon was desperate because an armada of hundred thousand was completely ready to leave but waiting for his decision only, so he accepted this grim offer at the expense of his daughter's blood. We learn from "Iphigenia" by Euripides that Iphigenia was brought to Aulis on the pretext of marrying Achilles. When Agamemnon's wife Clytemnestra and daughter found out about this sinister plan, they were petrified. When Agamemnon was about to sacrifice his daughter, Artemis spared her by ascending her into the sky and sending a deer instead of her. God Artemis's anger subsided and the wind began to blow. They set sail from the Port of Aulis and sailed guided by King Telephus of Pergamum on the right route to Troy. They went straight to the Lemnos Island (Limni in Turkish). They rested there for a while and then went to Tenedos (Bozcaada) and subdued it. As we learn from Sophocles' tragedy

Temple of Apollo Smintheus in Chryse (told in the Iliad) in the vicinity of Troy. Uncovered after a five-year excavation by the author of this book.

"Philoctetes", while sacrifices were being offered to Apollo Smintheus for this victory, Philoctetes was stung by a snake. Philoctetes was one of Helen's suitors and he joined the expedition to Troy when he was called out, with 20 ships. He possessed the famous weapons of Heracles. The wound caused by the sting of the snake became festered and began to spread an unbearable smell as it deepened. Therefore, Odysseus and his friends had to leave him on the island of Lemnos. Philoctetes lived here on his own for 10 years. However, Troy was not going to fall without the weapons of Heracles. Thus, Odysseus went to Lemnos and deceived him and brought him to Troy.

A thousand ships carrying the Achaeans cast anchor at the Port of Bashika near Troy. They stayed here for a long time, launched raids from there to nearby locations and capturing spoils. During one of these raids, Achilles went to Lyrnessus, captured the already-married daughter of the Priest of Apollo, Briseis, and killed her husband.

As the Achaeans continued to plunder the Troas coast, Achilles was plundering the city of Chryse near Cape Baba. Chryseis, the daughter of the priest Chryses of Apollo, was captured here, and when the spoils were being divided, she fell to the share of Agamemnon. Iliad tells of the last 51 days of the ten-year war, and this legend made up of 24 chapters begins with the priest of Apollo wanting his daughter back, and ends with the death of Hector.

THOSE WHO CAME FROM ANATOLIA
TO HELP TROY

The Trojan War, which was reportedly caused by a problem stemming from the abduction of a woman, is a theme from Homer's Iliad, one of the most influential epic poems in the world. The Iliad tells only of the final 51 days of the Trojan War, which lasted for 10 years, and ends with the death of Hector. The Trojan War, which is told in not only the Iliad and Odyssey of Homer but also in Virgil's "Aeneid", has also been proven by archaeological evidence. It can also be said that this war, which is known as the first battle between the East and the West, could have actually emerged due to more serious incidents than a mere problem of abduction of a woman.

Around 1200 BC, when the Achaeans under Agamemnon's command came to capture Troy with 1,000 ships and an army of 100,000 men, subsidiary troops from many places of Anatolia came to help Troy. These were at the disposal of 27 principals and kings, led by Hector, the son of King Priam. When recounting those who came to help Troy in the Iliad, Homer gives priority to Dardanians, who had kinship with Troy. They were led by Aeneas, whose fame was comparable to Hector's. Next, Homer mentions the inhabitants of Zeleia among the assistance troops that came to Troy. They were led by Pandarus, the son of Lycaon, and lived upon the slopes of Ida and were those who drank the limpid waters of the Aesepus. Zeleia is located near Lake Sarıgöl in the present-day district of Gönen. Homer also mentions the inhabitants of Adresteia and the land of Apaesus. He states that they were on the steep slopes of Tereie, in Pityeia, led by Adrestus and Amphius. He adds that they were both the sons of Merops of Percote. Then, the inhabitants of Percote came to help. Percote was located 10 km. north of Lapseki where the Bayramdere stream flows into the sea. After the 5th century BC, the inhabitants of Percote moved from here to the vicinity of the village of Sindal, which is 4 km. from Umurbey.

Next, Homer mentions the inhabitants of Sestos and Abydos. Sestos was situated in the cape of Akbaş near Eceabat across from the Dardanelles Strait and is famous for the love story of Hero and Leander. Across from here lies Abydos, which became well known after the Persian Emperor Xerxes had a bridge formed from his ships and had his army cross to the other side over that bridge during his expedition to Greece in 480 BC. The inhabitants of Arisbe, which was to the west of the region of Troas, also came to help. Homer later mentions that the Pelasgians, under the

Modern-day Amazon statue from Terme, Samsun.

command of Hippothous, provided assistance as well. Their city was known as Larissa. Another Thracian tribe, known as the Ciconians, came under the leadership of Euphemus. Yet another Thracian tribe, the Paeonians, came under the command of Pyraechmes.

After these, Homer mentions those who came from further afar. This is how he tells of the Paphlagonians:

"The Paphlagonians were commanded by stout-hearted Pylaemanes from
Enetae, where the mules run wild in herds. These were they that held Cytorus and the country round Sesamus"

As is known, Paphlagonia was an ancient region with lands opening to the Black Sea. Sesamus was located on present-day Amasra.

Commanders of the Halizoni who came to Troy from the Black Sea were Odius and Epistrophus. The Mysians, who dwelled near the present-day Balıkesir, were led by Chromis and the seer Ennomus. After this, the Phrygians came to Troy from Ascania. Having lived in a disorganized manner, the Phrygians only became a state around 750 BC. Although their legendary king is known as Midas, he is referred to as Mita in the old Assyrian documents. Their capital was Gordion near Ankara and their open-air temples are located between Eskişehir-Afyon.

The Meonians came to help Troy under the leadership of Mesthles and Antiphus from the slopes of Tmolus, which is the present-day Bozdağ Mountain in Manisa.

"Nastes led the Carians, men of a strange speech. These heldMiletus and the wooded mountain of Phthires, with the water of the river Maeander and the lofty crests of Mt. Mycale. "

This is how Homer introduces the Carians, who came to assist Troy. The Lelegians, a branch of the Carians, also came for assistance. They dwelled on the Bodrum Peninsula and established many famous cities on the peninsula. Finally, Homer recounts the Lycians among the assistance troops.

"Sarpedon and Glaucus led the Lycians from their distant land, by the eddying waters of the Xanthus."

By stating that *"Sarpedon and perfect Glaukos commands the Lycians, they had come from the far Lycian countries, from Eddy Xanthos"*, he introduces the Lycians to us. Sarpedon was the most prominent figure of the Trojan War. He came from Lycia to protect the Anatolian lands against attacks, and fought fearlessly. There were times when the Trojans would

yield, but Sarpedon continued to fight without losing heart. In the Iliad, he rebukes the Trojans as follows, in an effort to encourage them again:

"Where is your prowess now? You used to say that though you had neither

people nor allies you could hold the town alone with your brothers and brothers-in-law. I see not one of them here; they cower as hounds before a lion; it is we, your allies."

When the Trojan War broke out, Sarpedon, the king of Lycia, came to Troy to protect the lands of Anatolia without expecting any gain. However, even his father Zeus was not able to help him avoid the hand of fate, and he died during this war. The Chief God called Apollo to take and burry his son to his country and commands to take his dead to his country. Thus, Sarpedon was brought to Lycia and buried there. Another group of warriors who came from afar to help Troy was led by Memnon, who of Trojan blood. Memnon is the protagonist of the epic of Aethiopis, which tells of the subsequent events of the Trojan War that the Iliad does not cover. This epic, which was written by Arctinus of Miletus, could not survive to the present time. Another group of warriors coming from afar were the Amazons, who fought on their bare-backed horses, wearing short dresses and with their hair flowing in the wind.

THE EPIC OF ILIAD AND THE TROJAN WAR

Iliad tells us of the last 51 days of the Trojan War, which lasted for ten years. The Iliad begins with the description of how the priest of the plundered city of Chryse, a city on the Anatolian side, asked for his daughter who was abducted by Agamemnon to be freed. Agamemnon refused his request by saying *"I will not free her. She shall grow old in my house at Argos far from her own home."* Then the priest prayed to his god Apollo to take revenge from the Achaeans by crying "Hear me, O god of the silver bow, that protects Chryse and holy Cilla and rules Tenedos with thy might, hear me oh thou of Sminthe." God Apollo accepted the wish of the priest and caused a plague epidemic in the army of the city, which raged for nine consecutive days and nights. When they asked the seer Calchas the reason for this, he said that the girl should be given to his father so that the anger of Apollo would subside. Agamemnon did not listen to this advice, but Achilles pressured him to give the daughter back. The two thus fell out with each other, and Achilles left the battle and returned to his barracks. Agamemnon's behavior hurt him deeply. His mother Thetis went up to Zeus and wished that the Achaeans should not see any victory until they apologized to her son. Zeus granted her wish, as well.

Finally, Agamemnon accepted to give back the daughter of the priest. He assigned Odysseus to this task. Agamemnon continued the battle thinking he could be victorious without the help of Achilles but had no success. The Trojan armies led by Hector pushed back the Achaeans to where their ships were. They almost burnt the ships. On seeing this, Achilles allowed his friend Patroclus to fight wearing his clothes. Hector fought Patroclus whom he thought was Achilles and took the weapons of Achilles by killing him. Achilles was deeply saddened by the death of his beloved Patroclus. He asked for new weapons from his mother Thetis. Thetis had the blacksmith god Hephaestus make new weapons and brought them to her son.

Equipped with his new weapons and forgetting about his resentment to Agamemnon, Achilles attacked the Trojans to take revenge for his friend. He killed everybody whom he came across, because no weapon was able

Vase illustration of the Trojan warriors Achilles and Aias while playing checkers in their free time. 540 BC. Vatican Museum.

Mosaic showing Achilles and his mother Thetis. Samsun Museum.

to hurt him due to his semi-immortal nature. This caused a great panic among the Troian troops. Meanwhile, Achilles and Agamemnon had made peace and a meeting of the gods was held in Olympus. Each god sought Zeus's approval to enter the battle on the side they supported. By the permission of Zeus, Hera, Athena, Poseidon, Hermes, Hephaestus entered the battle on the side of the Achaeans. On the other hand, Ares, Apollo, Artemis, Leto and Aphrodite sided with the Trojans. Thus, the war heated up notably with the entrance of the gods into the battle. The River God Scamander came out of his bed and began to chase Achilles, who had killed thousands of Trojans cruelly and whose grudge would not cease. However, the fire god Hephaestus stopped him with his flames. Thus, the gods began to fight tooth and nail. Meanwhile, Achilles pushed back the Trojans and came close to the city walls. He killed everyone who had failed to go into the city walls.

Thereupon, Hector stood against him. He began to fight Achilles without listening to the cries of his mother and father, and shot a spear at him. The spear broke in the middle when it was about to go into Achilles'

chest. Hector understood that his end was drawing near. Eventually, the blow of Achilles'spear struck him down. When Achilles was about to kill him with his dagger, Hector asked him to give his dead body to his father and breathed his last. Achilles undressed Hector, tied his naked body to the back of his chariot, and dragged his body around the city walls of Troy seven times. Before the eyes of his father Priam, his mother Hecuba and his wife Andromache, despite their loud cries, he continued dragging the corpse of Hector around the Trojan walls, with wild pleasure. In the end, he took the body back to his barracks. Even the gods could not stand this horrible scene. Apollo and Aphrodite guarded the dead body of Hector for days and nights, applying oils on it. Finally, they persuaded Achilles to give this noble dead man to his father Priam. Priam took the body of Hector and brought it to Troy. The death of brave Hector was lamented for nine days. Men piled up woods for nine days, and on the tenth day, they put Hector on this pile of woods and burnt him. Then the fire was extinguished, and the bones of Hector were collected and put in a golden box. Later, they buried this box and covered it with large masses of earth rising as if mountains. Thus ends the Iliad, but the war was not over yet. Many more events were to be experienced.

THE EVENTS AFTER ILIAD

Other poets discussed this subject from the point where Homer left. Among these poets were Euripides, Aeschylus, Sophocles and Virgil.

The Trojans buried Hector and returned to their city with pain in their heart. Exhausted and sorrowful, they began to work again to protect the Holy Troy.

Around this time, the Amazons, who dwelt on the shores of the Black Sea, came to Troy for help. Queen Penthesilea, who led these female warriors, now took the place of Hector as the commander of the armies. These female warriors, whose hair flowed in the wind and whose short skirts exposed their white legs, attacked the Achaeans by the command of their queen. Taken aback, the Achaeans were defeated. They chased them as far as their ships and confined them there. Meanwhile, Achilles, who was sitting by his friend Patroclus' graveside, saw the situation and encouraged the Achaeans. The Amazon Queen saw who encouraged the fleeing enemy, galloped her horse towards him, and passing through many people, stood before him. She shot her spear at Achilles, but the spear hit his shield and fell on the ground. This spear, which had pierced through many shields, failed this one time. The queen was shocked. How could she know that the shield was made by the gods? This time Achilles shot his spear, and it stuck into the right shoulder of the queen and made her fall off her white horse. Achilles pushed against his enemy and made the fatal strike with his dagger. When the helmet of his dying enemy came off, he discovered the outstanding beauty underneath. He was amazed and thought that this face could belong only to a goddess. Achilles had fallen in love with this beauty, who was breathing her last and whose cheeks were still pink and lips were half-open as if gently smiling. A single blow of Achilles killed Thersites, who laughed at his feelings and insulted the dead body lying on the ground. He then took the dead body to his tent, cleaned her wounds and gave her to Priam so that she could be buried with a ceremony that would suit her dignity.

The war continued at full speed. This time, helpers under the command

Vase illustration created by Eksekias in 525 BC, featuring Achilles' killing of the Amazon queen Penthesilea and falling in love with her after seeing her face as she fell on the ground. British Museum.

of Memnon came to Troy for help. The death of Achilles, who caused great distress to the Trojans, was drawing near as well. On one fine day, he was again destroying the Trojans by killing everybody he came across, penetrating fiercely through the Trojan soldiers. He came close the gates of Troy. Paris, who had not performed gallantly during the war before, pulled his bow and shot his arrow at him. The arrow hit Achilles' only vulnerable point, his heel. Black blood was sprouting from Achilles' heel, leaving the bravest man of the Achaeans in unbearable pain. Soon after, his huge body tumbled down like a pine tree. Aias and Odysseus were fighting with all their power in order to prevent the Trojans from taking his body. This time, Paris directed his arrow towards Odysseus. Seeing this, Aias threw a rock at Paris, which he picked from the ground, and the huge rock wounded and knocked him down. Meanwhile, they had taken the body of Achilles to their side. His mother and relatives lamented for him for seventeen days. Later, Achilles' corpse was burnt on a pyre. Trojans prisoners were killed as sacrifices for him. A tomb was built for him by the seaside and a mount of earth was dumped on it. Games were organized in his honor. His mother Thetis also participated in these games; she brought her weapons, which were made by the fire god Hephaestus, and declared that these weapons would belong to the one who did not allow the Trojans to steal her son's body. Voting was held and Agamemnon announced that the weapons should be given to Odysseus. Aias was very upset by this decision. He thought an injustice was being done because he deserved the weapons. At night, he decided to take his revenge from Agamemnon. While he was going to Agamemnon's tent, Athena deceived him, and he ended up killing the herds instead of slaying Agamemnon. When he recovered, he was so embarrassed that he killed himself. Aias was now dead too, after Achilles. Nobody had the enthusiasm and power to fight anymore. They consulted the seer Calchas. He said that Helenus, the seer son of King Priam of Troy, must be taken as hostage because he was the only one who knew how Tory could fall. Odysseus undertook this mission and finally brought Helenus from Mount Ida. They forced him to tell them how Troy could fall. For the fall of Troy, Achilles' son Neoptolemus had to come, the arrow and bow of Heracles had to be brought, and the statue of the goddess found in the Temple of Athena in Troy had to be taken. Neoptolemus was brought by his grandfather. Heracles' arrow and bow were with Philoctetes. Philoctetes had departed for the purpose of participating in the Trojan war, but on his way, his leg was bit by a snake on the Lemnos Island. When his wound worsened, his friends took him to the Lemnos Island and left him to die

Plate illustration from 500 BC, showing Achilles bandaging the wounds of Patroclus. Berlin Museum.

there. Cursing at Agamemnon every day, Philoctetes finally healed and survived by hunting. Odysseus and Achilles' son Neoptolemus deceived this angry Philoctetes to Troy. Sophocles tells of this theme in his "Philoctetes".

Meanwhile, the battle was going on at full pace. Achaeans were becoming completely hopeless. Neoptolemus had come and Heracles' weapons had been brought. However, Troy still did not fall. Meanwhile, Philoctetes shot Paris with one of the poisonous arrows of Heracles. They carried Paris into the city walls. The poison of Hydra on the arrowhead was spreading through Paris' body and leaving him in endless pain. By the evening, Paris' pain had become unbearable. Paris remembered his ex wife nymph Oenone living on Mount Ida. Only she could heal him. They took Paris to Mount Ida, Paris begged her to forgive him and heal him, but Oenone would not forgive this man who had once abandoned her and refused to apply the balm that would heal his wound. Thus, Paris, the real cause all of these events, died. Oenone killed herself after him. On the other hand, the Achaeans' hopes were about to end. The goddess Athena suggested an idea to Odysseus for conquering Troy. This idea was to construct a wooden horse.

Odysseus immediately accepted the idea suggested by Athena. A huge horse was going to be built and the Achaean heroes were going to be hidden inside it. They were going to tell the Trojans that they had given up the fight and this wooden horse was a gift for them as the reminiscent of the war. When the Trojans took the wooden horse inside the walls, the soldiers hiding inside the horse would come out, open the gates and let their soldiers into the city walls, which they were not able to surmount before.

They took action immediately in order to perform this idea. They cut down long trees and brought them from Mount Ida. A master named Epeios began to build a huge horse from these logs. He designed a huge space inside the horse where twenty soldiers could hide. He placed large stones on its manes and eyes, so the awe-inspiring horse became ready within three days. He left the horse's mouth open so that the people inside could breath. The bravest of Achaeans like Menelaus, Philoctetes, Neoptolemus, Odysseus and Diomedes went inside the horse. Epeios hid the rope ladders as well. They left a person named Sinon near the horse, boarded their ships, and began hiding behind Tenedos. Screaming with happiness, the Trojans ran to the coast when they saw the Achaeans packing up their tents and leaving by their ships. All that was left was a wooden horse. They observed this horse in astonishment, trying to find out what it was. They saw Sinon, who was tied to the foot of the horse. They untied him and asked him what the horse was all about. As previously planned, he explained that this horse was a peace gift for the Trojans, which they should take inside; otherwise this could upset the gods. He played his role well and convinced the Trojans. They began to discuss about accepting the horse inside the city walls in order not to annoy the gods. However, Laocoon, the priest of the Temple of Apollo, knew that this was a trick and was trying to warn the Trojans. He shot his spear towards the paunch of the horse, which hit one of the Achaeans. His friends had shut his mouth to prevent noise, so nothing could be heard. The Gods had made the decision for Troy to fall. Therefore, nobody listened to Laocoon. In fact, Poseidon sent two snakes and had Laocoon and his sons suffocated. All of these events encouraged those Trojans who wanted to accept the horse in order not to offend the gods, so they decided to take the wooden horse in.

Wooden horse figure on a large vase created around 675 BC.

They brought the wooden horse near the city walls after tying it with ropes. However, they had to destroy the gate on the west because the huge horse would not fit. Thus they took the horse inside and began to celebrate by chanting and dancing around the war gift. Only Cassandra, Priam's daughter, said that this was a trick and cried out that it was going to bring a disaster. Nobody listened to her because they were drinking and celebrating the end of the ten-year war. At night, everybody was drunk and went to their homes to sleep peacefully for the first time after a long while. They fell into a deep sleep. The only person who did not fall asleep was Helen. For many times, she had been told to leave Troy to stop the war, but she did not leave. After Paris' death, she married Deiphobus, the brother of Paris. She did not trust the Achaeans and thought that this was a trick. She had strange feelings about this wooden horse incident. She got out of her home and came near the horse. Helen mimicked the voices of the Achaeans' wives one by one and called out their names. She was good at impersonating. When she called out for Anticlus, she did it so skillfully that Anticlus thought it was his wife calling and wanted to respond. However, Odysseus shut his mouth so tightly that Anticlus suffocated and died. Still suspicious, Helen wandered around the horse for three times and eventually went back home. When she was entering her home, Sinon secretly left the house, in which he was being hosted as a guest, and came near the city walls. He lit a fire on the walls as a sign to the Achaeans in Tenedos. Then, he told the soldiers inside the wooden horse to come out. They took their places one by one, killed the guards of the city walls, and opened up the gates.

Meanwhile, the forces hiding behind Tenedos had come too. They were now entering Troy, which they were unable to capture for ten years, with the help of a wooden horse. They began a slaughter, which lasted until the morning. They were destroying, burning and killing Trojans cruelly in their sleep. The holy city of Troy was burning in the flames. Priam's daughter Cassandra had taken shelter in the Temple of Athena by this time. She was trying to save herself by embracing the statue of Athena. However, Aias, the son of King Oeleus of Locris, entered the temple right after her. He captured Cassandra and raped her. The Achaeans had become this shameless and ravenous.

Prince Aeneas was trying to stand against them with a handful of soldiers. Achilles' son Neoptolemus was now forcing through the gates of Priam's palace. Finally, he broke the gate and entered in. Old Priam, who had stopped using weapons a long time ago, was trying to defend himself, but his weak body was losing its power every passing minute. His wife held his

Sculpture group showing the priest Laocoon (who proclaimed that the wooden horse was a trick and should not be accepted into the town) and his sons being suffocated by the snakes sent by Poseidon. Vatican Museum.

arm and, with difficulty, brought him near the altar of Zeus in the courtyard of the palace. Women and children had all gathered here.

Priamos' son Polites was wounded and ran away, and Neoptolemus was chasing him like an angry bull. In the end, he caught him and killed him before his father's eyes. With the last remaining strength in his body, the old king attacked Neoptolemus but Neoptolemus struck him down just by one blow of his sword. They cut his head off and dragged his body along the beach. Priam's wife Hecuba and their children, together with thousands of Trojan women and children, were captured and Helen was found where she was hiding and was taken to the beach. All the treasures of Troy were gathered under the porches of the Temple of Athena. Only Prince Aeneas had survived, and he was trying to save his father and wife. His wife was dead; he took his father on his back and carried him to a deserted place.

Meanwhile, the survivors of the slaughter had come there. Aeneas was trying to save the lives of those who were with him, escaping towards Mount Ida. They were going to build a ship and migrate to a new country on it. Hector's ill-fated wife Andromache was captured too and was being dragged from city walls to the beach with her child in her arms. The little child was crying continuously as if he was sensing this horrible situation. Odysseus took the baby from his mother's arms and threw him from the city walls.

Even the gods could not stand what they were doing anymore. One day, they were going to pay a price for what they did. Achaeans, who could not take Troy through bravery but by a simple trick, had devastated the city. They had nothing else to do, so they gathered on the beach so share the spoils and the noble women of Troy. The Trojan women were gathered in a tent. At that moment, the Trojan Queen Hecuba saw her little daughter Polyxena being sacrificed by the graveside of Achilles. How could a mother's heart stand this? Her pain would not subside. To add to that, she soon found out that their friend King Polymestor of Thrace, to whom she had entrusted her son, had killed her little son. The desire for revenge stiffened her heart. Senility had weakened her. However, her heart as a mother resembled that of a lion. It was time for her to take her revenge. Hecuba invited the Thracian king and his sons to the tent where the Trojan women were gathered. How could this man, whom she hosted at her home several times and regarded as friend, had turned his back on her after the fall of Troy? Soon after, the Thracian king came with his sons. Hecuba asked him about her son and the gold she had entrusted to him.

He told her that her son was growing up in his palace. Thereupon, they killed the liar king's sons before his eyes and blinded the king. Euripides mentions this in his "Hecuba".

Hecuba then went on to uncover the lies of Helen, who was trying to make it up to Menelaus. She had asked her to leave Troy to end this devastating war, several times, but Helen was telling her ex-husband that she wanted to come back to him but she was not allowed to leave. Menelaus believed in her lies and caressed her.

Troy was not going to give in, so the Achaeans thought of the wooden horse trick and conquered the city. This wooden horse, which was constructed when the author of this book was Director of the Çanakkale Museum, has become the symbol of Troy today.

THE LEGEND OF AENEAS AND
THE FOUNDING OF ROME

The Aeneid written by the Latin poet Virgil opened a new era by serving as a bridge between the Antiquity and the Middle Ages. In this work, Virgil found a source for his national culture by taking the past of Rome as far as Troy, and adding a new national depth to it. In this epic tale which tells of the events subsequent to those in the Iliad, the main hero was the Trojan Prince Aeneas, who was the son of the goddess Aphrodite and Anchises.

One decade passed with all the violence continuing in the Trojan War, and troops coming from many parts of Anatolia were fighting bravely with the Trojans. Aeneas, who led the Dardanians, also joined the conflict. He was wounded in the hip during his single combat with Diomedes, after which his mother goddess Aphrodite removed him from the battle field. The city, which did not fall from the war, fell from the plot of wooden horse placed within the city walls, which devoured the city in flames.

Aeneas moved out of the city together with his father, son and some of his friends, by taking the advantage of darkness in the alleys of the burning city and with the help of Aphrodite. His wife, who was following them, was kidnapped by the Mother Goddess Cybele. Aeneas began to seek her in the city without knowing she had been kidnapped. Later, when his wife in a dream said that he should go to find a new country, he left together with his companions. The events following this were narrated in Virgil's "Aeneid".

Aeneas left together with his companions. They barely reached the piedmonts of Mount Ida, where Aeneas gathered the dispersed Trojan soldiers. They did not know where to go and where to build a country. He was told in his dream to go to Hesperia in the west of Italy with his companions and Aeneas told his friends to be prepared for a long journey. They began to build, with full force, the ship which would take them to their country. They sailed to the deep seas on their ship, taking with them the Penates, who were their household deities, and their holy offerings. As they left Troy, they wept bitterly.

While the Trojans sailed under the leadership of Aeneas, they first took a short break in Samothrace and then reached the shores of Macedonia and

The gate of Troia (Troy) VI and the street behind it, where the war took place.

Embossment depicting the Trojan shepherd Anchises and Aphrodite holding Eros in her arms. The moon goddess Selene was shown as watching them.

Thrace, then Crete, Delos and Cythera, and later Laconia and Arcadia. During these journeys, they first encountered the creatures known as the Harpies, which were birds with the face of a woman. However, they stayed away from these creatures and thus avoided any trouble.

After sailing for many days, on the Epirus coast, they came across the Oracle Helenus, who married Andromache, the widow of the Trojan hero Hector. Helenus advised them not to set foot in the eastern part of Hesperia and to settle in the northern part. Aeneas and his companions were all ears, and listened to this advice. Soon they set sail and came to an island where the Cyclops lived. When they disembarked on the island,

Embossment depicting Aeneas fleeing Troy. Aeneas is wearing a piece of armor and is carrying his old father Anchises on his shoulders while holding the hand of his young son Iulus.

a man ran towards them and said "I am one of Odysseus' sailors". Like you, we had come to this accursed island. We had fallen into the hands of the one-eyed Cyclops and some of us died. Odysseus and his colleagues were able to barely escape, but they forgot me here. I saved myself from being eaten by the Cyclops by hiding behind the trees. Therefore, he said "go away from here immediately, you are in grave danger". The Trojans sailed again and took the tired man with them.

Days on the sea began to pass by calmly. While they were turning at the cape of the island of Sicily, they were caught in a furious storm. This storm was the work of the goddess Hera because Hera hated the Trojans who were still standing. When she saw a handful of Trojans on the coast of Sicily, she went to Aeolus, the wind god, and wanted him to send his winds here. This was the reason for the storm in which Aeneas was caught.

When the waves were about to swallow them, the god of the seas, Poseidon, felt pity for them and sent Aeolus a messenger in order to calm the winds. The messenger said, "calm these winds, otherwise Poseidon will pull you to the bottom of the seas together with the island of the bronze palace". After this threat, Aeolus calmed the winds. But the winds threw them far from Hesperia and they went ashore in the city of Carthage in Continental Africa, where a queen named Dido lived. During this time, Hera thought of many tricks to make Aeneas stay.

The queen of Carthage received these tired and sick people with open arms, fed them and provided beds for them. The Trojans told the kindhearted queen everything that had happened. Aeneas and his men were living happily in Carthage, in Dido's palace. Meanwhile, the queen fell in love with Aeneas. Hera wanted Aeneas to stay in Carthage and his mother Aphrodite wanted her son to leave there immediately and face his fate. Therefore she wanted help from the god of gods, Zeus. Zeus called messenger god Hermes and said, "Go to Carthage immediately and remind him of what I say". Hermes found Aeneas and told him, "The chief god sent me to you. He ordered me to remind you that you should accept your fate in order to build a new city to replace your country, which was destroyed and burnt up". Aeneas decided it was time to leave. The queen felt sorry for this decision, and even though she begged so much to deter him from his decision, Aeneas did not give an inch. In the end, the queen cursed him and killed herself.

The Trojans witnessed large flames behind the city walls, while they were leaving the city by their ships. These were the flames of the burning Queen Dido's corpse, who could not stand this separation. The journey passed smoothly from Carthage to the coast of Sicily and they came to the city Cumae. Here, there was a cave in Lake Avernus through which Hades, the land of the dead, was accessed. Aeneas wanted to talk with his late father's soul here. He obtained help from the Cumaean priestess Sibyl for this. They went down to Hades together. Aeneas hardly met with his father and told him "I came here to learn my future from you and act accordingly", to which his father replied, "Your future seems bright. You are going to establish a new city and this city is going to be a very big country in due time". After this, he told him what to do in order to obtain victory in Italy, the difficulties awaiting him one by one. He came back to the surface of the earth together with the priestess Sibyl.

Together with Trojans waiting for him, Aeneas reached the mouth of the Tiber River the next day by following the Italian coast towards the northwest. They battled with the local Rutulian people here. Later, Aeneas left some of his friends, and reached the city of Palatine by continuing to proceed inland. Palatine Hill was the place where the city of Rome was to be founded. King Evandrus, who came from Greece, reigned in these lands. The King welcomed Aeneas in a friendly manner and after he hosted him, he sent Aeneas near his friends whom they had left behind, together with his son Pallas and a small navy. When he reached the mouth of the Tiber, with the help of his friends and the new coming powers, a battle was won against the Rutulians. At the end of the war, King Turnus of the Rutulians gave his last breath in the hands of the Trojan hero. And so, the epic ends here.

History books helped us to understand the following events and the foundation legend of Rome. According to this, the king embarked to Latium where a king named Latinus reigned on a plain near the mouth of the Tiber River. Here he married with his daughter Lavinia. His son Ascanius, whom he rescued from the fire in Troy by grabbing his hands, built his own city named Albalonga. Descendents of Ascanius reigned here for many years. Rhea Silvia, a descendent of Procas, was a nun in the Temple of Vesta. She made love with the war god Mars. From this, twin children named Romulus and Remus were born. When the king learned the situation of his daughter for whom marriage was forbidden, he threw the mother into the Tiber River and left the twins in the river by placing them into a basket. The waters dragged the basket towards a beach, where a she-wolf breastfed the children who were later raised by a shepherd.

When the twins grew up, they decided to establish a city near the Tiber River where they had been dragged to the beach. But the brothers had a falling out, and Rumulus, killed Remus. Rumulus then established the city of Rome on the Palatine Hill. They accepted many people to the city and married with neighboring women in order to increase the city population. Thus a community was formed in this newly founded city. Romans consider the date of city's foundation as the 21th of April, 753 and believe that they are descended from the Trojan race.

GLOSSARY

Achilles: The son of Peleus and Thetis, a hero who joined the Trojan War.

Agamemnon: The king of Mycenae, brother of the Spartan King Menelaus, and Commander in Chief of the Achaeans joining the Trojan War.

Aias: A hero from Salamis who joined the Trojan War.

Amazons: Legendary female warriors with a single breast, who lived in Northeastern Anatolia.

Ambrosia: The food of the gods, which ensured immortality and healed wounds.

Andromache: The wife of Hector the Trojan hero.

Aphrodite: The goddess of love and beauty, who was known as Venus in Latin mythology.

Apollo: The son of Zeus and Leto, brother of Artemis, and the god of light, fine arts and foresight.

Ares: The son of Zeus and Hera, a war god. He was known in Latin mythology as Mars.

Argonauts: The brave sailors of Argo who went to the land of Colchis on the Black Sea in quest of the stolen golden fleece.

Ariadne: Ariadne first fell in love with Theseus, who came to Crete to combat Minotaur, and later married Dionysus the wine god.

Artemis: The daughter of Zeus and Leto, sister of Apollo, and goddess of hunting and virginity. She is known in Latin mythology as Diana.

Asclepius: The son of god Apollo and the god of health.

Astyanax: The son of the Trojan hero Hector and Andromache. Odysseus killed this child by throwing him off the walls of Troy.

Atalanta: A huntress symbolizing Artemis around the Arcadia region of Greece.

Athena: Athena, who was born from the head of Zeus, was the god of intelligence and war. He was known in Latin mythology as Minerva.

Atlas: One of the three sons of Titan Iapetus and Clymene, who was the daughter of Oceanus. He was punished by the gods to carry the earth on his back.

Bacchae: Female followers who observe the religious ceremonies of god Dionysus.

Bellerophontes: The hero who killed the flame-breathing monster Chimera, riding his winged horse Pegasus.

GLOSSARY

Cassandra: The daughter of Trojan King Priam and his wife Hecuba. She was cursed by the god Apollo for not returning his love; she was able to foresee future but her words would not be believed.

Centaurs: Mythological creatures with the upper part of their body resembling a human, and the lower part a horse. They lived on mountains and in forests.

Cerberus: The scary hound which guarded the land of the dead.

Ceres: The Roman goddess of soil and the products of soil.

Charites: Goddesses who symbolized things that appealed to the eye. They were known and depicted as the "three Charites".

Chimera: A monster sprouting flames from its mouth.

Circe: The daughter of Helios and Perse, Circe was a famous mythological female magician.

Cronus: The son of Uranus and Gaia.

Cupid: Latin counterpart of Eros, the god of love in Greek mythology.

Cyclopes: The children of Poseidon and Amphitrite, who were singleeyed giants.

Daedalus: An Attican, Daidalos reportedly came from a royal lineage and was the father of Athenian craftsmanship.

Daphne: A nymph whom Apollo fell in love with, and who later turned into a myrtle tree.

Dardanus: The son of Zeus, he built the Trojan castle. The Çanakkale Strait, which was formerly known as the Dardanelles. This term derives from Dardanus.

Demeter: The goddess of the fertility of the earth and the harvest. Her counterpart in Latin mythology is Ceres.

Dionysus: The son of Zeus and Semele; thegod of wine.

Dioscuri: The name given to Zeus's twins Castor and Polydeuces.

Eos: The goddess of dawn, shown as the sister of Helios (Sun) and Selene (Moon).

Epimetheus: The son of Iapetus and Clymene, whose name means "the one who thinks after the fact".

Erinyes: Goddesses who spread vengeance.

Eris: The goddess of strife.

GLOSSARY

Eros: God of love, son of Ares and Aphrodite. The only child god among the gods.

Europa: The daughter of King Agenor of Phoenicia, one of the wives of Zeus, who also gave her name to a continent.

Eurydice: She was the wife of Orpheus the bard, an was an oak nymph.

Fortuna: The goddess whom Romans feared and revered the most and who symbolized "blind fate".

Gaia: Mother Earth. She was the oldest goddess, who gave birth to Uranus and later married him.

Ganymede: He was the son of the Trojan king, was abducted by Zeus to Olympus, and became a cupbearer to the gods there.

Gigantes: The giants created from the blood spattered by Uranus's cut-off genitals.

Golden Fleece: The fur of the winged ram which was abducted from Greece to the land of Colchis on the Black Sea.

Gorgons: Evil mythological creatures that had snakes for hair and scary glances.

Griffins: Mythological birds with eagle heads and lion bodies.

Hades: The god of the underground land of the dead.

Harpies: Mythological birds with a woman's face, broad wings, sharp claws. Their name means "snatcher".

Hecate: A benevolent goddess, she was the guide of those suffering hardships.

Hector: A Trojan hero, son of Priam mentioned in Iliad.

Helen: The wife of the Spartan King Menelaus and the cause of the Trojan War.

Helios: The son of Hyperion and Thea, he was the all-seeing god of sun.

Hephaestus: The son of Zeus and Hera, god of fire and blacksmiths.

Hera: The wife and sister of Zeus. Her counterpart in Latin mythology is Juno.

Heracles: The son of Zeus and Alcmene, famous for achieving the twelve labors given by Hera.

Hermaphrodite: A type of human who has both feminine and masculine attributes.

Hermes: The son of Zeus and Maia, he was the courier and messenger

GLOSSARY

of gods. His counterpart in Latin mythology is Mercurius.

Hesperides: Nymphs of the location where the sun sets.

Hestia: The daughter of Cronus and Rhea, goddess of "hearth an home". Her counterpart in Latin mythology is Vesta.

Hippolyte: Amazon Queen who was killed by Heracles.

Hippolytus: The son of Theseus and an Amazon.

Horae: The three daughters of Zeus and Themis, goddesses of time and seasons.

Hydra: Horrific mythological dragon-snake with countless heads.

Hygieia: She was the daughter and assistant of the health god, Asclepius, and at the same time the goddess of health.

Hypnos: The god of sleep, and the brother of Thanatos who personified death.

Icarus: The son of Daedalus and the master of artisans; he became famous as the first man on earth to attempt flying.

Iliad: Epic of the Trojan War written by Homer.

Io: Io, the daughter of an Argos king named Inachus; One of the wives of Zeus.

Iolaus: A hero participating in the voyage of Argonauts to seek the golden fleece.

Iris: The daughter of Thaumas and Electra. She symbolized the rainbow and dispatched news from gods to people.

Janus: A god guarding the doors of homes according to what the Romans believed. A god specific to Rome.

Lapiths: Gigantic mythological people who lived in Thessaly.

Leda: One of Zeus's wives, whom he tempted by disguising as a swan. Helen and the Dioscuri were born from this marriage.

Leto: The wife of Zeus and the mother of Apollo and Artemis.

Luna: Roman goddess of the moon.

Maenads: The female followers who observed the religious ceremonies of the god Dionysus.

Marsyas: A silenus who entered a music competition with the god Apollo.

Medea: The daughter of King Aeetes, who helped the Argo sailor Jason to capture the golden fleece, using her wizardry.

Medusa: One of the three Gorgon daughters of Phorcys.

GLOSSARY

Meleager: Aetolian hero who joined the Calydonian boar hunt.

Menelaus: A Spartan king, the husband of beautiful Helen, who was abducted by Paris and thus caused the Trojan War.

Metis: The epitome of intelligence, reason and wisdom, Metis was the daughter of Oceanus and Tethys, and the first wife of Zeus.

Minos: The legendary Cretan king, who was the son of Zeus and Europa.

Minotaur: The name of a monster with a bull's head and human's body, meaning the bull of Minos. He was killed by the gallant Theseus.

Moirae: The daughters of Zeus and Themis, the goddesses of fate.

Muses: They are the nine spirits of inspiration.

Nectar: A special drink for gods which made drinkers immortal.

Nemea: The name of one of the monsters (a lion) which was fed by Hera and killed by Heracles.

Nemesis: She was the daughter of the night, and the goddess of vengeance.

Neoptolemus: The son of Achilles, the Greek warrior.

Nereids: The name of the sea nymphs who were the daughters of Nereus and Doris.

Nereus: One of the old men of the sea, he was born from the union of Gaia and Pontus.

Nike: The goddess of victory with wings. Her counterpart in Latin mythology is Victoria.

Niobe: Niobe, the daughter of Tantalus, was transformed into a rock by Apollo and Artemis because she ridiculed their mother Leto for having a small number of children.

Nymphs: Spirits who were believed to have lived around mountains, forests, wilderness, springs and torrents.

Nyx: The goddess who symbolized the darkness of the earth (night).

Oceanus: The son of Uranus and Gaia, god of seas and waters.

Odysseus: King of Ithaca who joined the Trojan War and was renowned for his guile.

Odyssey: Epic by Homer which tells of the adventures of Odysseus on his return from the Trojan War.

Oenone: One of the nymphs on Mount Ida, the first love of Paris.

Orthus: The name of a dog born from the drakaina Echidna and Typhoon.

GLOSSARY

Pallas: An epithet of the goddess Athena.

Pan: The goat-footed Pan was the son of Hermes and the god of shepherds and the ovine.

Pandora: The first woman created according to Greek mythology.

Paris: The youngest son of the Trojan King Priam and Hecuba, who caused the Trojan War due to beautiful Helen.

Patroclus: An Achaean warrior who was killed by Hector during the Trojan War.

Pegasus: The winged horse born from the blood of Medusa.

Penelope: The wife of Odysseus, the protagonist of the epic poem Odyssey.

Penthesilea: A renowned Amazonian queen who was killed by Achilles during the Trojan War.

Persephone: The daughter of the goddess Demeter, who was abducted to the underworld by Hades.

Perseus: The son of Zeus and Danae, the mythological hero who killed the Gorgons.

Phaedra: The daughter of the Cretan King Minos, sister of Ariadne, and wife of Theseus while he was king of Athens.

Philoctetes: He is Heracles' friend whom he bequeathed his weapons before his death.

Polyxena: The youngest daughter of Priam and Hecuba. She was sacrificed beside Achilles's tomb.

Poseidon: The god of seas. His counterpart in Latin mythology is "Neptunus".

Priam: The last and unfortunate king of Troy.

Prometheus: The son of Iapetus and Clymene, who was known as "the one who thinks beforehand". He was punished for giving fire to people secretly from gods.

Psyche: Literally means spirit. Eros loved Psyche, who was a girl with bird-like or butterfly-like wings, but he caused several sorrows unto her.

Rhea: The daughter of Uranus and Gaia. She married her brother Cronus.

Satyrs: They are part of the retinue of Dionysus. They were legendary woodland deities symbolizing nature. The part of their body above their waist was shaped as a human, and below as a horse and goat.

GLOSSARY

Scylla: The scariest of the sea monsters together with Charybdis.

Selene: The goddess of moon, sister of Helios and Eos.

Silenus: A company of Dionysus. It was a half-human and half-animal creature resembling satyrs. The difference between them was that Silenus was older.

Sinon: The spy whom the Achaeans left near the wooden horse while withdrawing from Troy.

Sirens: Legendary creatures with a woman's body, bird's wings and beautiful voice. They were a big threat to sailors.

Sphinx: A winged creature with the chest and face of a woman, and the body of a lion.

Telemachus: The beloved son of Odysseus and Penelope.

Telephus: The son of Heracles and Auge, and the hero of a dramatic story.

Tethys: The daughter of Uranus and Gaia, wife of Oceanus and goddess of all rivers.

Thanatos: The personification of death. The child of Nyx, brother of the god of sleep, Hypnos.

Thea: A female titan, who married Hyperion. She bore Eos, Selene and Helios.

Theseus: One of the greatest heroes of the Greeks.

Thetis: The wife of Peleus and the mother of Achilles.

Titans: The children of Uranus and Gaia. Titan means giant.

Triptolemus: An Eleusinian hero who features in the legend of Demeter.

Triton: The son of the god of seas, Poseidon, and Amphitrite.

Tyche: One of the daughters of Oceanus, who was the goddess of luck and coincidence.

Uranus: The name given to sky, personified as the primordial father of the first generation of gods.

Zephyrus: The son of Astraeus and the goddess of dawn, Eos. The west wind.

Zeus: The greatest of the Greek gods, The chief god. His counterpart in Latin mythology is Jupiter.